Kids These Days

A Teacher's Inspirational Journey That Will Change the Way You Think about Today's Youth

Mary Endres Thomas

Scripture verse from the following translations:
New American Standard Bible (NASB)
New International Version (NIV)
King James Bible Version (KJBV)
New King James Version (NKJV)
New Living Translation (NLT)

Printed in the United States of America

Second Edition, 2016

ISBN 978-0-9978986-0-6

Cover design and layout by Howell Printing

Howell Printing
345 Barnwell Ave., NW
Aiken, SC 29801
(803) 6489-2545

www.howellprinting.net

Dedication

As years of memories were beginning to evolve into a manuscript, I would often reflect upon an individual who has been the most influential teacher in my life. As I completed the first draft of each chapter, I quickly printed it out, mailed it to this amazing woman and then anxiously awaited her critique. I chose to send them to her because I knew her feedback would always be positive and encouraging; two very important ingredients for this first time author to continue to move forward in this lofty endeavor. Although I was confident of the significance of the many stories that I held within my heart, I was not as confident that I possessed the ability to adequately relate them so that others might be as inspired by them as I had been. This woman's enthusiasm, encouragement, and hunger for the next chapter were often the motivation I needed to sit back at the computer and continue this quest.

As she received each new chapter, she would call and we would reminisce about those days gone by. She would always ask for the latest updates on these now adult former students. She knew each of the young people I had written about in the early chapters and she cared for them as much as I did. She knew their stories, she knew their challenges, she knew many of them personally because I shared their stories with her as they unfolded so many years ago.

She is the reason I became a teacher. I wanted to share that same wisdom, strength, encouragement and compassion that she had shared with me and countless others throughout her 93 years of living. I prayed that I would have that same positive life changing effect on those I would encounter on my journey just as she had done with me. She has truly been an inspiration to all who have had the privilege of knowing her.

I chose to dedicate the writing of this book to Mrs. Bernice Endres, my first teacher, my mentor, my friend and most importantly, my mother.

Acknowledgments

First and foremost I give all praise honor and glory to God, my Lord and my Savior.

Thanks to my husband Joe Thomas, whose ears were the first to hear each chapter as the rough drafts were completed. Joe also was one of my biggest cheerleaders throughout the past 30 years as many of these chapters were actually being played out.

Thanks to my daughter, Christy, who never complained of my time spent away from home due to my involvement with so many school activities. I want to thank her for all the times she tagged along with me to assist with the projects. Thanks for her involvement and the leadership role she played when she became one of my "Kids These Days". Christy is such an inspiration to me, as well as the many who are privileged to know her.

Thanks so much to my siblings and their families, who upon discovering I was taking on this endeavor, flooded heaven with prayers, and me with much verbal support throughout this venture.

Special thanks to my brother Gerry Endres, who encouraged me many years ago to write this book. He has always expressed an interest in my students and enjoyed hearing my many stories. He had encouraged me for years to share these stories with others. Gerry put a thought in my head that wouldn't rest until this book was complete. It was Gerry's belief in me that gave me the confidence to even begin this undertaking. He had a front row seat throughout the writing of this book; reading each chapter as scores of notes and memories began to formulate into comprehensible stories. Gerry was always supportive both prayerfully, as well as constructively critiquing my work.

There are always behind the scene kind of people who prove to be invaluable in the completion of such a lofty goal as this. Thanks so much to my brother Frank Endres who immediately fell in love with the idea of this book. He called several times a week always prompting, always inquiring, always encouraging, and always wanting to read more. During those times when the words would not flow, when ideas were slow forming and sitting in front of the computer was tedious; it was Frank's phone calls and his excitement that re-energized me. He helped to keep me excited about continuing, and completing this book. Frank actively began promoting this book before the last chapter was even written. I wasn't certain sometimes if it was excitement or his failure to take his thyroid medicine; regardless, his fervor generated the confidence and enthusiasm I needed to complete this project.

Another such supporter was my best friend, Janet Zimmermann. When I first uttered the idea of writing this book, Janet began encouraging me to do so. She believed in me, she believed in the stories that were to be told. Janet and I were walking/jogging buddies. Throughout the 18 months of the writing of this book Janet and I logged in over 2,500 miles. During these workouts, Janet patiently listened as I rambled through decades of teaching memories to verbalize ideas into chapters for this book. In addition, Janet supported me spiritually as she prayed for the success of this book, as well as, take on the task of selecting scripture quotes for the completion of each chapter. I want to express a very special "thank you" to Janet, my friend, my confidant, and my sister in Christ.

Special thanks to one of my – kids these days - David Estep who was just a phone call away whenever I needed tech support and help with the photos. He is an amazing young man, always ready to be of service.

There would be no book without the tremendous cast of characters whose stories are shared in the following chapters. I have estimated that I have taught, coached, and/or been club advisor to over 7,000 students during my teaching career. Every summer, before a new school year began, I would pray that God would send me the students that he wanted me to have. Therefore, each one of you is an answer to a prayer. Whether your name is mentioned in this book or not you have been a tremendous inspiration and blessing to me. Each one of you is one of my "Kids These Days" (and my mom thought she had a lot of kids ☺). Collectively, you have made me the person and the teacher I am today. I thank you all for an amazing career that I will always cherish.

Contents

Foreword

Kids These Days is a book about improvement and the impact a professional educator can have on so many. It depicts the influence amazing young folks, though often hurt, limited and challenged with seemingly insurmountable obstacles, become inspirations to their peers and the adults who set out to help them. This book takes an optimistic look at youth and the process of making positive changes.

Within these pages are stories of students whose interests and focus moves from typical teen self-orientation to caring for and serving others in need. The book tenderly shares the personal commitment and satisfaction derived by these students as they learn the value of service to others through assisting victims of tragedies, family members, the elderly in nursing homes, and peers in need.

I have been privileged to have known and worked with this author and have observed her incredible skills at relating to students and extracting the best of their creativity, talents and courage. However, the stories told here gave me a far greater appreciation of her passion and love for her students, her remarkable tireless energy and her skilled detective work, resulting in solutions for so many troubled individuals.

The stories told here are true and any one of them alone is so extraordinary as to have made the author's career worthy and influential. Students like the ones so realistically described exist in all communities and schools and are waiting to be discovered, loved, respected and empowered to become far more than they ever dreamed possible. Many are waiting to be shown how to dream. This author is the "real deal" as a teacher/coach and she has, by example, so ably imparted how others can recognize students whose lives can be changed by a caring person willing to invest energy, creativity and time beyond the standard school day.

Kids These Days reflects the power and influence embedded in the teaching profession which can effectively be used to change the lives of students and others. It should be encouraged reading for middle and high school students, college students preparing for a teaching profession or a career in the social sciences, and seasoned educators needing a refreshing reminder of why they do what they do and how they might do it differently. Readers should be prepared to be entertained, flooded with emotions and inspired by this book.

William A. Gallman, Ph.D. (Retired)
Psychologist
Deputy Superintendent: Aiken County Public Schools

Preface

For the past forty years, when meeting new people and casually conversing with them, I have often been asked what I do for a living. Upon hearing my "schoolteacher" reply, a typical response is, "Wow, I feel sorry for you!" followed by "What do you think about these kids today?"

I retort, "Don't feel sorry for me, I love my job. Feel sorry for those who are trapped in jobs they detest."

I discovered, when attempting to respond to their inquiry, people do not really want to hear about kids these days unless I can predict the next newspaper headline about how out of control they are. "Kids out of control," a very small percentage of our teenagers, yet they receive the most publicity.

I would like to invite you to take a four-decade journey with me so that I might be able to share what I have been privileged to witness about *Kids These Days*.

In the beginning...

This was new to me. I had been summoned to report to the principal's office. This really wasn't too surprising. However, the reality of facing the principal was a bit unnerving. My pace slowed and my heart raced as I neared the office. It was time for me to face the inevitable. I went over this scenario numerous times, anticipating her every question and practicing my responses. Not really certain what to expect, I nervously reminded myself to take a deep breath as I clasped the doorknob. Opening the door, I stepped into an unfamiliar waiting area. The secretary motioned for me to sign in as I glanced around the spacious room, trying to take it all in, wondering even then what she thought of me. As I turned to take a seat, I was surprised to see two of my close friends already settled in and waiting their turn for obviously the same reason. No words were spoken. We only had a chance to exchange a nervous glance before the secretary instructed me to proceed to the office where my fate awaited me. The principal's office door was open. As I stepped through, she closed the door behind me, and thus began the interview process for my very first teaching position.

She clasped my hand, introduced herself, and instructed me to sit in an oversized leather chair as she walked around her massive desk and sat in what I perceived as her throne. She was tall, slender, had dark hair, and seemed so eloquent. She spoke softly, and her quiet demeanor had a calming effect on my rapid heart rate. Her inquiries were more related to my personal life than my education. My large family rather than my GPA was of more interest to her. I immediately felt a sense of calm as my interviewer began questioning me. I was much more comfortable talking about family than Piaget's theory of intellectual development. After engaging in what I thought was random conversation for about twenty minutes, she stopped taking notes and lay down her pen. She seemed to be pondering something for a moment, and then she rose from her chair as she began to speak. I quickly stood as well. She approached me, saying, "I just have a real good feeling about you. I think you are exactly who I'm looking for. The job is yours." I couldn't believe what I was hearing. As soon as I met her, I knew I wanted to work with her. There was a connection between us that I could not explain, and apparently she felt it as well. She spoke again, saying, "However, you have to promise me one thing. I still have two more people to interview (she was referring to my college buddies in the waiting room); you cannot let on that you already have this position." We embraced, and she challenged me to bring my feet back down to the floor and walk out as though I knew nothing, a task that was much easier said than done.

Teaching jobs were hard to come by during that time. Neither of those friends was able to acquire a teaching position that school year. I felt truly blessed. I was on top of the world! I knew I was ready to begin my much-anticipated teaching career. My student-teaching experience at the local high school was eye opening as well as a tremendous confidence builder. I had a bachelor of science degree in mathematics education with a minor in English. I was young. I was enthusiastic. I was committed to make a difference in the lives of young people. I was ready!

It didn't take long to see that my ultimate goal had a major flaw. The kids! I was teaching junior high school kids who couldn't care less about algebra and geometry. They did not share my enthusiasm for their success.

There was quite a blend of students. It seemed everyone from the county was represented at this inner city school—black, white, those from the hollers, those from the hills, the haves and have-nots, those in mansions, those from the projects. Life was tough for many of these kids, and they didn't mind making it tough on their teachers.

The veteran teachers cautioned me about many of these children, knowing that I would be challenged as a rookie. I believe that through divine intervention, it just so happened that as I was entering this school to teach, my younger siblings were moving from here into the high school. Students were quick to make a family connection with our unusual last name of "Endres." My siblings obviously left an impression on my students because the first question from many was, "Are you Jude's sister?" or "Are you Joanie's sister?" I was proud to say yes. More than once I overheard students say, "Don't mess with her, she's Jude's sister," or "She's cool; she's Joanie's sister." I guess you can say that I basically got a free pass from some of the most challenging students. I love my family!

I thought often about my job interview and the questions that she pursued. I began to realize that the education I received in college was not near as important as the education I first received at home. This lady knew these kids, and she knew what they needed. I would never teach quantitative analysis, differential equations, or even calculus. However, through her questioning, she discovered I possessed something more important that these kids disparately needed—the basic life skills that were taught in my home.

My education began long before I started school. I did, however, come from a very privileged upbringing. Quite spoiled, I thought. I had everything! I had parents who loved me along with my twelve siblings. They taught us about love by showing us love, and that with love comes responsibility, respect, and sacrifice. We learned very early that life was not about us (except on our birthday ☺)—it was about how we could be of service to others. They instilled in us a strong belief in God—Father, Son, and Holy Spirit—I'm sure it took all three of Them to raise thirteen children! They empowered us with a strong work ethic and a belief that we could be successful in any endeavor. Oh yes, we were rich. We had everything except money. Being number eight, I learned later in life that when paychecks were scarce, the older siblings worked to fill in the gaps. There was never a need to turn to the government for assistance because there was a tremendous support group through church, neighbors, friends, and, most importantly, each other.

When needs seemed to exceed existing funds, my mom would turn to Scripture. I recall that one of her favorite Scripture passages where she drew much strength and wisdom was from Matthew.

"For this reason I say to you, do not be worried about your life, as to what you will eat or what you will drink; nor for your body, as to what you will put on. Is not life more than food, and the body more than clothing? Look at the birds of the air, they do not sow, nor reap nor gather into barns, and yet your heavenly Father feeds them. Are you not worth much more than they? And who of you by being worried can add a single hour to his life? And why are you worried about clothing? Observe how the lilies of the field grow; they do not toil nor do they spin, yet I say to you that not even Solomon in all his glory clothed himself like one of these. But if God so clothes the grass of the field, which is alive today and tomorrow is thrown into the furnace, will He not much more clothe you? You of little faith! Do not worry then, saying, "What will we eat?" or "What will we drink?" or "What will we wear for clothing?" For the Gentiles eagerly seek all these things; for your heavenly Father knows that you need all these things. But seek first His kingdom and His righteousness, and all these things will be added to you. So do not worry about tomorrow; for tomorrow will care for itself. Each day has enough trouble of its own."

Matthew 6:25–34 (NASB)

I witnessed firsthand throughout my life the power of giving to others: my parents opening their home to those in need, feeding homeless who would come to our backdoor, ministering to the sick, ministering to the dying, volunteering midnight shift answering the telephone at an emergency crisis center, as if raising thirteen children wasn't enough. I recall one brother purchasing my high school class ring for me, knowing that neither I nor my parents had money for such extravagances. Another brother paid my tuition my last semester of college because I was unable to work my two part-time jobs and do my student teaching. Giving, with no expectation of anything in return, was the environment in which I was raised.

Even with a family this large and everyone going in different directions after school, we all always gathered together for the evening meal. We not only said grace before each meal, but Dad had us recite the "St. Francis Peace Prayer." I thought it was pretty cool when I finally learned all the words and was able to recite it along with my older siblings. However, after years of saying these words, it seemed that's all they were—just words. I couldn't have been more wrong. What I didn't understand at that time was that because we recited that prayer so often, those words became the fibers that formed the very fabric of our lives. I can see today in each and every one of my brothers and sisters the manifestation of this prayer.

"St. Francis Peace Prayer"

Lord, make me an instrument of thy peace,
Where there is hatred, let me sow love;
Where there is injury, pardon;
Where there is doubt, faith;
Where there is despair, hope;
Where there is darkness, light;
Where there is sadness, joy.

O Divine Master, grant that I may not so much seek to be consoled as to console; to be understood as to understand; to be loved as to love; for it is in giving that we receive, it is in pardoning that we are pardoned, and it is in dying that we are born to eternal life.

—Saint Francis of Assisi

I received an amazing education from amazing teachers. This is what my principal soon challenged me to share with these children.

Kids these days

"For I know the plans I have for you," declares the LORD, "plans to prosper you and not to harm you, plans to give you hope and a future."

Jeremiah 29:11 NIV

 **Chapter 2**

My First Challenge

I don't think that my early days in school were much different than other people's. I recall those first days of school when I wrestled with myself about even getting out of bed. I debated the whole going-to-school thing. I didn't want to go—the kids were mean, most of the adults seemed mean, school lunches were terrible, I hated doing homework, I missed afternoon naps, I missed spending time with my mom, the list went on. I pondered if there was even one important reason why I should get up and go to school? Oh yeah, I am the teacher; I really should be there.

I was reminded of a gift given to me by my best friend from college who also was experiencing the same first-year-teacher trauma. Susan had given me a cardboard cutout of a sad little dachshund puppy saying, "Just when I learned all the answers, they changed all the questions." How appropriate! I just thought I learned everything I needed in college. The age-old educational theories did not prepare me for kids these days. Every day I seemed to be challenged with a different issue in the classroom on top of all the teenage drama. Life was interesting to say the least.

So many kids coming and going every day in my classroom, it took a while to learn names and faces. However, there was an unfamiliar face that kept showing up in my doorway between classes. A student, who was not in any of my classes, would often walk by and simply glare into my classroom at me. It was a bit unnerving to say the least. I once overheard one of my students tell this stranger as she snatched her by the arm, "I told you she is okay, leave her alone." That vote of confidence did not deter this young lady from making every effort to intimidate me.

In my inquiries about her, I discovered her name was Benita but went by Pee Wee. I thought this to be a very unusual nickname for such a daunting personality. I heard a litany of problems that other teachers had experienced. I guess you could sum up most of her issues by saying she lacked respect for authority, and apparently most of the rules shouldn't apply to her. This simply created more questions—why her obvious dislike of me? I was new; she didn't even know me. Perhaps that was the problem. I was new, haven't been tested yet; this was her territory and perhaps I crossed the line.

After a couple of weeks of baptism by fire, I once again found myself in the principal's office. Sitting in that leather chair, I was contemplating the numerous mishaps of the past weeks as they were flashing through my head. While wondering which one we would be discussing, she broke the silence stating that there was something of urgency that we needed to discuss. Now my pulse raced as I wondered if I still had a job. She made reference to our initial encounter and a topic we discussed during the interview. She asked if I was sincere about coaching girl's basketball. Relieved that my job was not in jeopardy and anxious to please her, I assured her I would be glad to assist another in this endeavor.

The coaching responsibilities that she had in mind were vastly different than mine. I discovered immediately that I would be *the* coach and not to count on an assistant. When I informed her that playing P-I-G in the alley was the extinct of my knowledge of basketball, she did not waiver. However, she promised that she would get me some books on the game. She concluded stating that anyone who grew up with eight brothers should be able to handle this and encouraged me to ask them for additional assistance.

Wow! I was not sure where to begin. There had never been a girls' basketball program at this school. Actually it was relatively new at all the junior highs in the county. I was so proud that she trusted me with this incredible responsibility, especially after what I perceived as a shaky start, at best, in the classroom. However, I soon discovered that for two years administration had been trying to get this program started, and I was simply the first to say yes.

I knew whatever I did would be an improvement on what was currently being offered, but I was committed to doing this right. More than anything, I wanted my principal to be proud of me. My number one question still remained unanswered: "Where do I begin?"

At that time in our state, the girls' basketball season ran simultaneously with football season. This provided better access to the gym if the girls and boys had consecutive seasons. However, this created an urgency to get the ball rolling, so to speak. It wouldn't be long before the first game, and I didn't even have a team.

I decided an obvious beginning would be to announce this new opportunity for the young ladies at the school. I, as well as other teachers, talked it up in the classroom, and the principal made special announcements to the student body.

Tryouts began immediately, along with my education of the game through the use of books and brothers. In addition, I quickly understood the desire of the administration to get this program in place. It was a wonderful disciplinary tool for keeping these players out of trouble. There were many challenging students whom they personally encouraged to join this newly forming team. Their plan—give them something special that they can threaten to take away.

On the first day of tryouts, I hurried to the gym after my last class to find sitting on the bleachers the most diversified group of young teenage girls imaginable. I quickly discovered that their playing ability was just as unequivocal. I rolled out the basketballs and began the process of choosing a team.

There she was! What was she doing here? That same hate-filled glare, that same intimidating attitude, not just toward me but to many of the other players as well. I wondered why Pee Wee even chose to tryout. This seemed to create an additional challenge to getting a team together; keeping the team together.

Pee Wee was taller than most of the girls and was quite muscular in build. This young black girl had a good knowledge of the game and played aggressively. I appreciated her talent but still questioned her motive to be on the team. Her eyes screamed of hate as she glared at me.

Even after the team was chosen, there remained tremendous diversity and playing ability among the girls. We worked hard for weeks on basic skills, dribbling, passing, and ball handling. Each day more rules of the game were introduced and incorporated into the workouts. Each practice brought with it a greater level of confidence and an enhanced feeling of team.

I have to admit that I was putting more time and effort into this extracurricular activity than I did into my teaching. After all, I was confident in my knowledge of mathematics; basketball is where I was deficient.

I soon felt an additional responsibility with many of the girls on my team. After a few days of practice, I discovered that many did not have a ride home. Some lived close enough to walk but others lived clear across town. They were bussed past one junior high school to this one so they could keep a proper ratio of black and white students. Because they stayed for practice, they always missed the school bus and many just did not have someone they could depend on for a ride home.

Luckily, this was a time before seat belt laws and restrictions on number of passengers because I would have all the kids without a ride pile into my car (a two-door, four-seater) for a ride home—all the girls, except for Pee Wee who still did not trust me. When the others hollered for her to jump in, she rolled her eyes and turned away. I'm not certain how she got home, but I was confident that she knew how to survive on the streets. Many of the girls lived in federal housing, and as I approached that development, the girls would not let me drive into the project. They insisted that I drop them off at the entrance and they would walk to their respective homes. I wasn't sure if they were embarrassed by the living conditions or concerned for my safety. Either way, it was a sad place to call home.

Finally, it was game day! Along with that arose another problem—getting the team to the game. With several phone calls, I was able to recruit a few parents to assist with the transporting of the team. I wanted the starting five to ride with me; there was still so much I wanted to tell them. After all, with only six of us in the car, there was far more room than usual.

This was the first "real" basketball game that any of us on this team had ever experienced. Lots of mistakes were made. I did not have my scorebook ready. In fact, I did not even know how to keep the book. I was unfamiliar with pre-game drills and team protocol. All I knew was we were ready to play ball. Just tell us which basket is ours and let the game begin. The officials soon did just that. The excitement was uncontainable. Mistakes did not end with pre-game. Luckily the opposing team was just as nervous and plagued with as many mishaps. With the end of each quarter, the team ran to the sideline looking to me for direction. We discussed strategy and went back onto the court. The score was very low and very close as the lead changed hands numerous times. The quarter was over, the girls ran to huddle, encouraged that we were leading by three points. Again we were discussing our game plan when the official joined our huddle and said with a grin, "Coach, the game is over! Congratulations! You won!"

Anxiety was quickly exchanged for excitement, and then, for the very first time, when our eyes connected, Pee Wee smiled at me. What a beautiful smile. She looked like a different person—she was a different person. We not only were victorious on the court that day, a much more important victory took place: I won her trust.

Years later, I heard John Maxwell's quote, "People don't care how much you know, until they know how much you care." My mind raced back to this time, to this place, to this situation where that quote was not just words on a page, it was a life-changing reality.

I began to witness an amazing transformation of an angry, troubled, seemingly uncaring person to a young lady who suddenly had a purpose. She was part of a team, not just a player, but a leader. She became a motivating force in getting this program off the ground. Teammates no longer followed Pee Wee's lead due to fear but, rather, respect. As an eighth grader and throughout her freshman year, she became a vital participant in the building of not just this program but also the girls' athletic program in general. She went on to letter in three sports each of those years.

When the administration asked me to deal with her now-diminishing discipline issues, her excuses quickly turned into apologies as Pee Wee realized I wasn't going to tolerate mischievous behavior. One raised eyebrow on my part brought out her sheepish grin and a promise to do better. She became a positive influence on many troubled students in the classroom as well as the sports arena. She became a leader by example. Given the opportunity, she chose to give up the street and move onto a highway of success. She not only joined us on the rides home, Pee Wee asked to be dropped off last so we could talk about anything, about everything.

With a promise that I would always be there for her, she graduated high school and attended college. After a couple of years in college, Pee Wee called me one evening and asked if I could assist her with tuition. She wanted to stay in college but did not have the means to do so. Honoring my promise from nearly six years previously, I immediately told her I would. I was single at the time, with very little monetary obligations, so the decision was not difficult. However, I wanted her to understand the responsibility of borrowing money and the obligation of paying it back.

After our conversation ended, I began thinking how sad it was that I was the only adult in her life that she could turn to for such a request. I prayed for her future. I prayed for her success. The money was not important, but her future was. Whether I got the money back or not was of little concern. My prayer was that she pay this gesture forward, that she in turn would help others in need.

My thoughts wandered back, recalling the tremendous challenges that Pee Wee faced shortly after completing high school. At nineteen years of age, she gave birth to a beautiful baby girl. For the first time in her young life, as she held her infant daughter in her arms, Pee Wee truly understood the meaning of unconditional love. Tragically, when this child was only twenty-five days old, she died of SIDS (sudden infant death syndrome) which left behind far more questions than answers. Pee Wee was devastated beyond belief. Sadly enough, the heartbreak did not end here. Months later, her dad died unexpectedly from what seemed at first to be a minor injury.

It wasn't long after getting a job, Pee Wee began making monthly payments in an effort to repay her debt. Even when I moved out of town, she would visit my mom with payments to send to me. However, as had happened way too often in her young life, tragedy once again played its devastating hand. Pee Wee's mother died without warning of a massive heart attack.

At the age of twenty-five, this young lady had reached near breaking point, feeling that she physically and emotionally could not take anymore. When she had an opportunity for a better job out of state, she took it along with the balance of the unresolved debt. The money was not an issue for me. She certainly needed it far more than I. Her success was my concern.

For more than two decades, it was as though Pee Wee had vanished from the face of the earth. I continued to wonder about her knowing that life had always been a tremendous challenge for her. I prayed that she found the support and strength needed to deal with life's toughest blows.

It was while this book was far more dream than substance, I made an effort to re-connect with Pee Wee. My youngest sister informed me that Pee Wee was on Facebook and the rest is history. I sent her a message and the relationship was instantly renewed. I quickly discovered that she now prefers to be called Benita or BB, which are her initials.

While we were catching up, Benita shared with me that she would not be alive today if I had not intervened in her life. She was on a dead-end road of destruction. She did not pretend that life was easy into her adult years. The street often haunted her and still tempted her to return. Benita made some bad choices along the way, but she arose from those mistakes a stronger woman than ever.

She shared with me that her goal in life was to reach out to others as I had to her. She took on the responsibility to raise a couple of young boys who were brothers and whose mother was incarcerated. Benita provided a home for these boys into their late teens and did all in her power to give these youngsters what their mother never did. She provided them with a safe, clean, loving environment. She gave them a home where they learned the importance of trust and responsibility. Most importantly, she provided them an opportunity to succeed.

She volunteered with a foster care program where she visited many kids often. They begged her to take them with her; she cried because she couldn't. For months, she saved money from an inadequate paycheck to take numerous children on special vacations. Once Benita rented a twelve-passenger bus to take a group of children who previously never left their state to go to Disney World for a week. Another group went on Amtrak and even slept in sleeper cars in preparation for their visit to Las Vegas and then on to New Orleans for Mardi Gras. She continues to give these children hope and a reason to believe that they are special, and that someone truly cares about them. She has given them the best gift of all—a belief in themselves that they can be successful.

She has become a strong Christian woman who continues to have a positive influence on all those around her.

So, all these years later I have discovered that the debt was paid in full ten times over. She had indeed paid it forward.

Kids these days

"The thief comes only to steal and kill and destroy; I came that they may have life, and have it abundantly."

(John 10:10 NASB)

Learning the Value of Team

I kept that promise that I had made to myself when I first decided to coach the girls' basketball team. I became a student of the game. I read books, studied offenses, defenses, inbound plays, and strategies. I talked with the boys' basketball coach and gained tremendous insight. I knew the rules as well (and sometimes better, I think) as the officials. I attended coaching clinics, always improving my knowledge of the game. I knew if I expected the girls to be the best that they could be, I needed to do the same. I needed to be someone whom they respected as a coach, teacher, and mentor.

I knew early in my coaching career that the relationship with my team went far beyond the sport. These girls needed to be a part of something special—they needed to be recognized for accomplishments, they needed a reason to come to school, they needed to know that someone cared about them, they needed to be a member of a *team*. Being a part of this team provided all of this and so much more.

I put my heart and soul into this team, each year improving on the last. I made team booklets for the members that explained all of our plays. Everything was diagramed out so any novice could understand it.

In addition, I put inspirational and motivational quotes in the book; quotes that emphasized the importance of sportsmanship, teamwork, positive attitudes...After all, the football team had their playbook, it only seemed right for us to have one. Somehow it just made us a little more special, a little more authentic. As the years raced by, many of my previous athletes shared with me how much that book meant to them. One mentioned that she kept it just under her bed so she could pull it out each night and look through it. Another player shared with me that years later, she reproduced her book and gave it to players on a team that she was coaching.

Practices became more intense, drills became more involved, and additional offenses and defenses were introduced. The players always stepped up to the new challenges. Attendance at practice was rarely a problem. In fact, the girls often asked if we could practice on Saturdays. These practices were a treat because often my brothers would come work out with us. After Saturday practice, it was not unusual to play touch football. This was the only sense of belonging that some of these girls ever experienced. I can't express enough how diverse these teams were each year. However, I believe that it was this incredible difference that made them so close.

Many of the girls had wonderful families and parents who assisted with transporting these girls. They had mothers with whom I shared tremendous friendships. Other girls had nice homes but families who were too busy to even come to a game. Some girls had nothing. It was that common goal, that team spirit that made them one. We were black, white, poor, and rich (rich did not mean monetarily—not in this school district—it meant that you were blessed with a family who really cared) all coming together for a common purpose.

I guess every team has a song that inspires them; their rallying cry; a team's song that takes them into battle, so to speak. A song that is sung before each game that inspires them to victory. Our song? Sister Sledge's "We are family; I got all my sisters with me." I cannot think of a greater way to express their oneness as a team than the bond of sisterhood. To this day, I cannot hear that song without thinking of so many of those young ladies.

In an effort to build team pride, I, along with the girls, dressed up for each game. Everyone in school knew when it was game day not because they had a schedule. It was the unusual event where these young ladies would be wearing something besides jeans. This pride spilled over into practice. The girls worked tirelessly on many aspects of the game. One thing they took great pride in was the pre-game warm-up. It became so choreographed that often the opponents would stop their own warm-up to watch ours. The pre-game drill was intimidating to many of our opponents, and we often started the game with a major psychological advantage.

I'm not certain if it was my idea or one of the players', but prayer before every game became part of our ritual. After everyone was in uniform, we had a quick team meeting reviewing our game plan, which was always followed by prayer. Even that became competitive—

players arguing whose turn it was to pray. Now that was a wonderful problem to have.

Through the years, the basketball teams enjoyed incredible success. We never had a losing season. Each year, the new seventh graders would replace the old ninth graders who were moving up to the high school as sophomores. Those remaining veteran players would always teach the new players the game, the procedures, the expectations, "the system."

This worked for everyone accept for one new arrival. I did not notice the defiance at first. What I did notice was that she was good. Not just good, she had the ability to be one of the starting five. She was quick, a great ball handler, and had a good shot. Tina was everything you would want in a player, except the attitude. For the most part she did as instructed, played well with the team, and was quite an asset. I'm convinced that even at her young age, her knowledge of basketball and her skill level exceeded mine. But that was a nonissue. I was still the coach, something in which she was occasionally having trouble.

The team was blessed with a lot of talent this particular year. We had performed exceptionally well all season. We had defeated every opponent except for that team of "rich kids" who go to school on "the hill." To my knowledge, this particular opponent had never lost a game. In fact, they enjoyed humiliating other teams by defeating them by large margins. The coach's nickname was "Digger" because she always took delight in burying her opponent. One of the male coaches at her school would always carry a shovel into the gym, just adding insult to injury.

Though we lost, we played very well against this team earlier in the season. It was arguably the best outing ever against this team. Now was our opportunity to avenge our loss. It was Saturday morning and we were playing the championship game in their gym. There was a standing-room-only crowd. For the first time, "the rich kids" actually had some competition. We felt like it was the "haves" against the "have-nots"; the privileged against the not-so-privileged. We could make a statement for all the other teams who were humiliated by this group. We were ready!

The game began. We were competitive. We were confident. We played so well. The game stayed close until the final buzzer. Throughout the game I called various players close to the bench to instruct them as to what I wanted them to do. The gym was so noisy due to the excitement and enthusiasm of the crowd; this was the only way to communicate with the players. It was the last quarter. The lead continued to change hands throughout the game. The young seventh grader committed a careless foul, and I called her over to the bench to talk with her while the other team was shooting a free throw. Mostly I wanted to calm Tina down, let her know that we were still very much in the game. When I called her to come to me, she turned her back and waved me off. That was a mistake too big to ignore.

I substituted in another player whose basketball skills were far inferior to the one I just pulled. I had Tina sit beside me on the bench for the duration of the game. She sat quietly, knowing her mistake. Other players looked at me as though I was crazy, but I did not relent. The game ended and once again we came up short. Many people questioned why I took her out of the game. The principal of the opposing school was astonished as she approached me after the game stating, "You could've won!" I just smiled, hoping with everything that was in me that perhaps in the long run, we really did win. Their questions remained unanswered to keep from embarrassing my young player further. Could we have won the game if she stayed in? No one will ever know, and at this point no one really cares. However, I believe something far more important happened that morning.

Tina realized that she was a part of something much bigger than herself. She was a part of a team, and on that morning, her team was not successful without her. She let them down. She knew. More than anyone in that gym that day, she knew. She and I never discussed that game. Two years later, I attempted to bring it up. She knew where I was going and immediately changed the subject, and I left it alone.

No, it was never discussed, but the change in her was amazing. A new relationship began to form—a new respect for authority, a new respect for team. A new leader emerged. I had witnessed such a transformation before, but this time I took such a gamble, and this gamble had a huge payload.

We did not lose a basketball game for the next two years. We enjoyed a dynasty, with this young lady at the helm. When we played the kids on the hill and had a comfortable lead, every young lady on the bench was privileged to play and be a part of history in the making. The starters gladly sat the bench and cheered for those who did not often have many opportunities to play. This game was especially sweet.

Through the next two years, I had an opportunity to get to know this young lady on a much more personal level. She shared much with me. At the age of six, her parents divorced, and desperate for a place to live, her mother moved the family into one of the federal housing projects. Life for her was difficult to say the least. Tina's mother worked hard, loved and cared for her, but soon found herself trapped in the projects. Tina had older brothers who often found themselves on the wrong side of the law. That just seemed to be the way of life for many who lived there. It appeared that the "projects" was a place where dreams faded, desire to set goals seemed pointless, expectations of responsibilities shallow, hope for success limited.

Tina learned very young that she had to be strong to survive. She created a tough shell and dared others to penetrate it until she became a member of a team. A wonderful group of people whom she soon learned that she could trust; new friends who genuinely cared for her.

She told me many stories of life in the projects, but

the one that I just couldn't get over happened one summer. A young, quite intoxicated white man drove into the projects apparently with a death wish. He began screaming the "n" word. Not just once, but numerous times to get the attention of as many people as possible. Well that did not take long. Quickly he was dragged out of his car and stoned to near death. Mothers began grabbing their children and running to shield them from the violence. She said she remembered, as a youngster, people picking up sticks and large rocks and pummeling him with these objects until his body was seemingly lifeless. Unable to ingest any more of this torturous event, she ran home never learning the fate of that man.

Another time as a freshman in junior high, she went home from school and the door of her apartment was ripped from its hinges. She was afraid to enter and stayed with a friend that evening. After hearing of this incident, I asked my parents if she could stay with them for a few days until things calmed down. Once again, as they did so often in their lives, they opened their home to someone in need. My parents attended many of our basketball games and knew all of the players. Actually, I believe having her stay was their idea.

Tina went on to high school and continued to play basketball, continued to improve, continued in her winning ways. As a junior her team went to the state playoffs and lost in the first round. However, after getting a taste of the playoffs, her team was relentless the following year with one goal in mind; a quest for the gold. This team went undefeated not only in regular season play but right through the playoffs. Tina was a member of the very first girls' basketball state championship team for her high school.

Her incredible basketball skills earned her a full ride to college where once again she enjoyed much success both on the court as well as in the classroom. Tina was that college's first female to ever win the Student-Athlete of the Year Award which also gained her Hall of Fame recognition at this institution.

This young lady called me not so long ago on her fortieth birthday. She shared with me that she loved life. She was married with two young daughters. Tina had moved to Florida after graduating college, and was teaching in a middle school and coaching basketball. Imagine that! She said that on this special day, she was calling because she wanted to thank those who had such a major impact on her life and had help to mold her into the person who she was today—a person of whom we both are very proud.

Once again, kids, in the most deplorable circumstances, step up and do the right things, given a little guidance and opportunities. Rather than making excuses because life isn't fair, or life was too hard, they begin making a difference in their own lives and then in the lives of so many.

Kids these days!

> "And we know that God causes all things to work together for good to those who love God, to those who are called according to His purpose."
>
> (Romans 8:28 NASB)

An Unwelcome Stranger

The years passed, the years were good…and then from out of nowhere *he* showed up. He was detested by all. He was deceitful, a liar, and a thief.

He robbed individuals, families, and entire communities. His mere presence changed lives in an instant. He brought with him sorrow, pain, and confusion.

He robbed the young of their future, families of their dreams, communities of their peace.

He was crafty and his tools of devastation were numerous. Throughout my teaching career, I have witnessed a multitude of devices he uses from his arsenal of destruction—the overindulgence of drugs or alcohol, a missed curve on a motorcycle, crossing the yellow line into a semi, misjudgment at a train crossing, inattentiveness at the steering wheel, a well-placed bullet, seeking adventure in a clay pit, illness… Nearly two dozen teenagers whom I can readily recall were victims of his cruel hand; students from three different schools, three different states. There was no consideration of academics, behavior, race, religion, or wealth. No prejudice was shown when selecting a target.

His methods are many; the results are the same. His name? Death!

This was something that I never saw coming, somewhat blindsided, I guess you could say. However, once it started, it happened much too often. Those of us left behind always uttered that same unanswerable question—why?

Students were always quick to turn to their teachers for answers. These tragedies have become teaching moments for me once I was able to maintain my composure. However, in several situations, I totally lacked the ability to control my emotions and simply cried with the students and/or family.

I have to admit that time has robbed me of the memory of many of the details of the numerous devastating events. However, there are some things that I'll never forget. The emotions that surround these tragedies are life changing.

There was an instance where one of my students took his own life on a Sunday evening. I knew I would need to be strong for my students. Monday morning as they began to gather in our first period class, I was a pillar of strength. I knew I could do this. I hugged students as they entered my room. The guidance counselor asked if I needed her assistance dealing with this tragedy. I assured her that we would be fine. Yes, I was fine. I was fine until I entered the room and saw his empty desk in front of my own, where someone had placed a rose.

At that point, I began to sob. I exited my room, went across the hall to the library, and asked the librarian to summon the guidance counselor. I quickly realized I could not handle this one alone.

As I went back into the classroom, I discovered I was not alone. Twenty-six others were waiting, feeling just as I did, ready to mourn our loss together. Together we shared a plethora of emotions and questions. The math books stayed closed that day, but I don't think a better lesson was ever taught to this group. We all changed that hour; we were different for what we shared. It is hard to explain, but the very personality of the class changed; we all felt it. It wasn't a change that lasted the day, or even a week. I think I can speak for all in that group that it was a change that was to last a lifetime.

The morning began, as many before, these two best friends riding to school together. The drive was so routine that perhaps the driver was not as attentive as he should have been. The vehicle he was driving began to drift across the yellow line, and there was simply no time to correct the mistake before colliding head on into an eighteen-wheeler. In an instant, this day was anything but routine.

Many of our students drove that same highway to school—many witnessed that devastating scene. One of the boys died at the scene, the other did not live much longer. It was said that one of the friends, realizing the imminent danger, leaned over and placed his body across the other in hopes of protecting his friend. When I heard this, I immediately thought of the Scripture verse, "Greater love has no one than this, that one lay down his life for his friends." (John 15:13 NASB). I never questioned the reality of this because it certainly seemed that would have been true of either one.

As could be expected, it did not take long for this news to penetrate the halls of our small high school where they attended. These guys were seniors and very involved in school activities so everyone knew them or certainly knew of them. Emotions were uncontrollable. Students and teachers alike were overcome with grief. Many people's first response was anger. They were angry with God. They questioned how a loving God could allow this to happen. I truly believe that the devil was celebrating the turmoil within our school. I believe he felt victorious in the loss of two wonderful Christians and the emptiness, the questioning, and the anger that was left behind.

The enemy's triumph was short-lived. Together, we were able to change our focus. Instead of grieving our loss, we began to celebrate the lives of these two very special people. It was through the help of these boys' amazing parents that we began to heal as a community.

These young men were a joy. They were always happy, wonderful Christian role models. The tremendous impact that they had on others was evident by the multitudes that attended the viewing, the memorial service in a packed high school gymnasium, and a standing-room-only funeral service.

In their short lives, they taught many of us that true joy is found through serving Christ by being a service to others. Many lives were changed through this tragedy. Believers and nonbelievers alike took another look at their own lives. We reassessed what is truly important and how precious life, friendship, and family are in our own lives.

These fellas were always together; each other's homes, in church, in the classroom, the marching band, numerous band events and competitions. Yes, they were inseparable in life as in death. Their viewings were together, the memorial service at the high school, as well as their funerals were together. I feel certain that they are living heavenly eternity together.

Most of the deaths of students came in an instant, which always leave behind the hollowness of missed opportunities, words left unspoken, emotions left unshared. However, on this occasion, death came at a slower pace caused by terminal illnesses.

I have wondered from time to time what I would do if faced with the reality of death in the near future. The "bucket list" has become a common phrase for things people wish to do as they contemplate their numbered days of life as we know it. What would be on this list?

Lists often consist of daredevil feats, glamorous places, exotic vacations, family and friends.

I remember as a student in junior high that this young man did not seem much different than his peers. He was a good student, well-behaved, a good athlete, and enjoyed life. He went on to high school continuing to be successful on many levels. He put much effort into his academics because going to college was his major ambition. He realized that going to college was an aspiration of far more students than who actually received that letter from the admissions office.

That spring he received two affirmations—his acceptance to the college of his choice and that the growth under his arm was indeed cancer and had already spread to the lymph nodes.

Having heard this news, the young man still insisted on attending college. His parents gave in to his request and did as tens of thousands of other parents did that summer. They made preparations for their child to live on a college campus. They prepared him with all the material necessities he would require while preparing themselves for a heartbreaking good-bye.

Communication home was limited. Long distance phone calls were expensive. This was a time (if you can imagine) before computers, e-mails, cell phones, Facebook and Twitter. His occasional calls home were to always assure his family that he was doing just fine. It wasn't until he lost his battle with cancer that his family and friends discovered the truth of his final semester at school.

Not being out of college very long myself, I remembered how many students abused their newly acquired freedoms of living away from home for the first time—the parties, drinking, late nights, sleeping in, missing classes...but not this young man.

He attended classes regularly, completed assignments, and stayed focused on the reason he was there—to get an education. Even when he knew his days were numbered and the cancer was robbing him of nearly all his energy, he never lost sight of his goals. When there came a time when he could only walk a short distance, he begged his buddies to get him to class. They literally carried him on their backs to honor this request. All the while, phone calls home always assured his folks he was doing fine.

This young man's bucket list simply consisted of integrity, honor, and responsibility.

I recently heard from a man dying of cancer that we don't get to choose how we are going to die...we only get to choose how we are going to live. My mind immediately raced back three decades to thoughts of this young fella and how he chose to live his brief life, and the example he was to so many.

In the book *The Butterfly Effect*, author Andy Andrews states, "What we do today affects outcomes forever."

Believing this statement to be true, I've often pondered as to how many lives were affected by that beautiful butterfly. I know my own life was greatly inspired by the way he chose to live his.

Kids these days!

"For to me, to live is Christ, and to die is gain."

(Philippians 1:21 NASB)

Chapter 5

Lessons Beyond the Classroom

I love teaching—the interaction with the students, the excitement when struggling students finally understand difficult concepts. It is so rewarding when statements evolve from "I can't!"—"I'll try!"—"I get it!"

The lesson planning, homework, writing test, grading papers is time well spent when failing students begin to succeed, when students trust you to take them to new challenging heights, when homework is no longer viewed as a punishment but an opportunity, when students begin to believe in themselves. I love the classroom!

Saying yes to coaching basketball opened the floodgates to numerous coaching responsibilities. In addition to basketball, I coached volleyball, track, and tennis. I coached the boys as well as the girls. Each year, throughout my tenure at this school, I coached three sports at the school and for several years coached city league softball as well. I discovered that the sports arena, whether gym, track, or field, is a classroom that always provides opportunities for instruction. I was able to challenge, motivate, inspire, and get to know these students on a much different level. Coaching provided teaching opportunities that I never experienced in a classroom. One such teaching opportunity occurred late in the spring during track season.

It didn't take long that day for me to hear that one of the members of the track team would not be going to the meet that afternoon. This athlete was sick and would not be able to compete. Track-and-field typically is an individual sporting event. However, the young lady who would be sitting this meet out was very talented. She was scheduled to participate in three running events, which is the maximum allowed for this age group. Without her, I needed to rethink who would be running her events, which would change nearly all the dashes and relays. This person missing affected nearly every sprinter on the team.

All day long various team members questioned the reality of the runner's illness. "She showed up for school; she should be able to run in the meet." "She doesn't even look sick." On and on and on it went. The complaints didn't stop there. It went on with who was running what and with whom.

Wow! I had never heard so much bickering. First they were second-guessing the young lady's health, now they are second-guessing my coaching strategy. I have to admit, I was shocked at these chain of events.

I did understand their concern. For years, the girls' track team had dominated their competition and had earned a reputation of excellence. This year and this team were no different. Each weekly meet we walked away with top honors. If the team was lousy, no one would have cared about the major changes, but that wasn't the case. These girls took this sport seriously. They were not happy with all the changes. This certainly took them out of their comfort zone. We were expected to win, and now they began to have their doubts.

After much thought and consideration of the girls' strengths and weaknesses, I felt that I had placed each of the runners in events that would allow us to be the most competitive for the evening's meet. However, attitudes of the team members made it obvious that they did not share my confidence or enthusiasm with the new strategy. The complaining continued from the school to the stadium. While walking up the stadium steps, the team was so engrossed in their self-pitying attitude that they missed it. They walked right past him without a second glance, without a thought.

Having coached track for numerous years and already had numerous meets this season, I was familiar with most all the people who attend the meets. However, I had never seen this person before. He was a handsome young man, late teens or early twenties, sitting in a wheelchair. What caught my eye was that young man was a prisoner of the chair because he had no legs. I pondered why this fella would be at a track meet, of all places. I had never seen him before, and I never saw him again.

As my girls staked claim to a section of the bleachers for the team to settle in for the next several hours, they tossed their gear around in an attempt to let me know that they were still very unhappy about the situation.

Observing this behavior, I could no longer contain my frustration with them. I demanded everyone's attention as I began to speak. I instructed them to look over my left shoulder and see the young man in the wheelchair. As their eyes shifted in that direction, there was a collective gasp. I went on to say that guy would love to be in the situation that they currently found to be so deplorable. I reminded them that each one of them has so much to be thankful for, yet their focus remains on complaining about a situation in which they were not comfortable. I shared with them my disappointment that rather than stepping up and confronting this challenge, they chose to already make excuses for an inevitable defeat. I stated my dissatisfaction that no one chose to step up and be a leader to accept this challenge of change and share my belief in them that we would still be successful in our endeavor and that there was no shame in not winning when we all gave the best we had to offer. I went on to say that anytime that life is tough, think of that guy in the wheelchair and think for a moment what a real challenge would be like. We all have so much, yet we complain about something so trivial.

The girls would not even look at me after my tirade. I instructed them to go to the field and stretch while I attended the coaches' "scratch session." Prior to every meet, the coaches would meet with the track meet official and report changes they wanted to make from the original entry form submitted at the beginning of the week. This meeting typically took twenty to thirty minutes because it was not unusual in a large meet for there to be many changes that needed to be recorded.

As I was coming out of the tunnel and heading back to our section, one of the opposing coaches got my attention and motioned to the field as she smiled, "New stretching exercise, Coach?" Wondering what she was talking about, my eyes searched for my team on the field. What I saw brought tears to my eyes.

The pre-meet stretching ritual was more about getting focused for individual events, together. Yes, it is very important that athletes go through a plethora of stretches before their event, but many would not be running for hours and would need to go through this routine individually prior to their event. Again, this stretching routine prior to the start of the meet is more about coming together first as a team before doing individual events.

What I saw? My girls on the field, in a circle, on their knees, holding hands, heads bowed in prayer. I was touched beyond belief. It had to be obvious to everyone in that stadium what these girls were doing. They did it anyway, not intimidated about what others might think. They realized the task ahead, and they were reminded whose team they were really on.

As the circle collapsed and the girls began preparing for their events, the complaining was replaced with cooperation. The newly formed relay teams went to the field practicing their baton exchanges and worked on their timing. One offered advice to another as they prepared to compete in their new events. Cooperation, camaraderie, competiveness is what I was surrounded with as the meet began and the evening unfolded.

Did my team score more points than the other teams? I honestly don't remember. I have long since forgotten the results of that meet, but what will be emblazoned in my memory forever is that every girl who wore our school's uniform was a winner that night.

As for that young man in the wheelchair, we never saw him again that evening, or at any meet after that. But in our brief encounter, he changed the hearts and minds of an entire team.

Kids these days!

"Not that I speak from want, for I have learned to be content in whatever circumstances I am."
(Philippians 4:11 NASB)

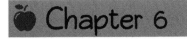

Chapter 6

After the Storm

It was the best of times, it was the worst of times... just kidding! I can't use this, someone else already did. However, this is somewhat a *tale of two cities*, so to speak, and the phrase captured some of the emotions I was feeling at this time in my life.

I just married my best friend. Joe had moved south nearly six months prior to our wedding for a wonderful new career opportunity, and now it was time for me to join him. I was leaving a job I loved, a community I loved, a church I loved, for the man I loved. I was excited yet anxious. I had lived in the same area for thirty-three years. I could not venture from home for more than a few minutes without running into a familiar face. That quickly changed as this mountaineer headed south to embrace a new adventure.

"South Carolina: Smiling faces, friendly places." I totally agree with this phrase that is embedded on the state's license plate. Southern hospitality is like none other. It didn't take long to develop new friendships and to be totally absorbed in a new teaching job that I cherished.

With all the changes I was making, I decided that I

needed to quit coaching to devote my energy toward my husband and, hopefully, children of my own. That changed within the first week of the new school year. I was asked to coach the girls' JV basketball team. I agreed to coach with the stipulation that it only be for the one season. That worked out fine because my husband was working second shift, so it helped fill empty hours in the evening. There were just two other coaching responsibilities that I agreed to for the remainder of my teaching career, and they were both the coaching of girls' tennis. I coached one season fairly early in my South Carolina teaching tenure and the other nearly two decades later. This final coaching duty was very memorable because as a senior, my daughter played in the number one spot. This team finished the season region champs, and my daughter, Christy, was the first female from this high school to play in the State Tennis Tournament. It was a true blessing to bring my coaching career to an end in this fashion. I had the pleasure of coaching the daughters of so many for so long, it was pretty amazing to coach my own daughter as I chose to hang up my whistle for the last time.

Well into the second year of this new job, the assistant principal approached me with a request to work with the girls' physical education teacher in an effort to start a Key Club in our school. A couple of gentlemen from the local Kiwanis Club had expressed an interest in sponsoring a Key Club on our campus, and this administrator was in search of advisors willing to be dedicated to the task.

I was always eager to help out, but I didn't even know what Key Club was. I quickly discovered that Key Club International is the oldest and largest service program for high school students. This club was to be led by the students with the goal to teach leadership by helping others.

This concept sounded pretty exciting to me. I had no problem making this commitment because I knew the PE teacher, Dru, would be a wonderful person with whom to work, and I was thrilled about the challenge of starting this new organization at our school. I was confident that it would not be as time-consuming as coaching responsibilities, and I did miss the extracurricular involvement with the students. I was ready for something like this. Little did I realize at that time what a life-changing decision I was about to make.

It was evident that the students were excited about this new community service organization; within a week we had about eighty students wishing to get involved. Our challenge as advisors was to create projects for this willing group of teenagers. By soliciting assistance from our new Kiwanis friends and a local Key Club, our organization grew quickly.

We all have an innate desire to belong, to be part of something, to be accepted, to be a member of a group. I believe that is why so many young people are quick to get into a gang. It fulfills that sense of belonging that they were not able to find within family, church or school. This club was an answer for those desiring to be a member of something. There were no prerequisites, no grade requirements, no special athletic talent; just a willingness to reach out and help others in need.

Year after year this club was strong. Typically there would be anywhere from 90 to 120 active club members. This represented about 15 percent of our school's population. This club was comprised of a very diverse group of young people. It was not just multiethnic, but athletes, special needs students, band members, every grade level, top of the class to its bottom, the rich and the poor...I was so proud to be a part of such a wonderful organization with such amazing goals, working with such committed youngsters.

It was midnight, September 22, 1989, when one of the costliest and most intense hurricanes to that date to ever hit the United States made landfall. Instantly, the lives of millions of people were literally turned upside down. Hurricane Hugo had blasted the South Carolina coast, where it slammed ashore just north of downtown Charleston. This storm produced the highest storm tide heights ever recorded along the US East Coast. Hugo bulldozed its way 200 miles inland to Charlotte, North Carolina, with 85 mph winds. Trees were uprooted, houses were crushed, many lost everything they owned.

The next day at school, Hurricane Hugo was the only thing that was on everyone's mind. Club members bombarded me with, "What can we do?" "We gotta do something!" Many were concerned about friends and family who lived in the path of destruction. We listened to the news for information regarding ways to help. Bottled water, canned food, clothes, personal hygiene items were on the top of the list. We encouraged all to donate, and the response was overwhelming. Dru housed this large collection of items in the gym. By week's end, numerous teachers along with their spouses volunteered to caravan these much-needed items to the coast, a two-hour drive away.

The new pastor at my church was recently transferred from the small island that felt the intense rage of this powerful storm. His most recent parish was where Hugo had made landfall. Father Joe helped us in coordinating our efforts to be of service to his community. He gave us names and phone numbers of people to contact who were coordinating efforts on the coast. Without this information, we could not even get close to those in need. Authorities in Charleston were making every effort to keep the sightseers and looters away to allow the needed help and those who had evacuated to come back home.

Every one of us have been appalled by pictures and video footage of massive storms and the devastation left in its path, but pictures pale in comparison with actually walking the streets and seeing the destruction; smelling the stench of dead fish, dead animals, and raw sewage. The look of despair, the tears flowing as people sort through the rubble that was once their home. Our task that day was to drop off our donations at the collection center, but my mind raced as I was thinking of all the work that needed to be done, the thousands of people who were faced with an impossible task of cleaning up after the storm.

The next week at school, when confronted with the challenge, the club members were unanimous in their decision to send work crews to this area. That Saturday, we filled a school activity bus with dozens of key clubbers and a few men followed in trucks with chainsaws, and we caravanned to the coast, not certain of our task, just knowing we wanted to help somehow.

Father Joe instructed us on the location of the volunteer station, and once we reported there and mentioned his name, they graciously welcomed us and then put us to work. Our large group was split into several smaller, more manageable numbers.

Mopping muddied floors was a task for a couple of our boys. If the wooden stick that they were handed had been a baseball bat, they would have known exactly what to do. However, their mops seemed to be quite foreign. I'm certain that this was the first time either one had even held a mop. After a few simple instructions, they were hard at work swabbing the deck. Several of the members stayed for that massive cleanup in their activity center. Dru and I took a large group to the residence of one of the parishioners of this small church. As my crew disembarked the bus, we could hear the voice of the fragile old lady on the front porch say, "God just sent me angels from heaven." This was the first day that people were able to get back to their homes because of fears of an unstable bridge. Ms. Sally had only been home a short while and was overwhelmed with the ruin she witnessed. She literally did not know where to start, nor did she possess the physical strength to deal with such a massive task. As we entered the house, it was obvious nearly everything downstairs was ruined. The water level in her house had reached several feet. We quickly began removing furniture, pulling up carpet, and removing appliances. All items were placed at the curb for pickup.

We all marveled at Ms. Sally's amazing attitude. She was so pleasant, so positive, and so tolerant of us throwing away so many of her possessions. A week later, we received a thank-you note from her, and she shared that just prior to our arrival she was in such despair. She told God that she could not deal with this alone; he needed to send her some help. She said as her prayers were being uttered, we arrived. At that point, her despair turned into hope and that she knew without a doubt that God was very much present in this disaster, and he would walk her through it. My kids felt encouraged by their efforts and couldn't wait to go back again.

After leaving Ms. Sally's, we went from one house and then another. The task was always the same, pulling up carpet and tossing garbage that was once valuable possessions. As we drove back to the volunteer station, the roads were like tunnels of debris. The curbsides were stacked high and long with lumber, siding, roofing, garbage, tree limbs, broken furniture, water-soaked sofas…all a long continuous reminder that an unwelcome intruder had paid them a very destructive visit.

The ride home was long because we were all exhausted, but everyone was anxious to share their group's stories and the devastation they had seen. There were houses that were lifted from their foundation and placed in the center of highways; houseboats were miles from the shore; dumpsters filled with dead fish from the storm surge; houses that were now just a pile of sticks; cars turned upside down; huge hundred-year-old oak trees uprooted; a palm tree that was like a spear dangling from the side of a building. For some, it was their first trip to the beach, they were seeing the ocean for the first time, but no one asked to go to the beach to walk along the shore; this wasn't the time. There was a job that needed to be done, and they began making plans to return.

I don't recall how many trips Dru and I made or how many different members and adult volunteers were involved but there are some situations that I will never forget. It seems every Saturday was sunny and hot as our tasks moved to the outdoors. Our job now was to help remove debris from yards, driveways, and roadways. Some of the men had chainsaws and they cut the large trees into much smaller and more manageable sizes to make this cleanup effort possible. Week after week the kids worked hard, only taking breaks for water and lunch. One day one of the girls worked herself to complete exhaustion and suffered a seizure. She was taken to the emergency room where they blamed dehydration and exhaustion for the episode. I had never before witnessed teens so totally giving all that they had. Everyone on every trip home was always totally spent, holding nothing back as we assisted in this exorbitant cleanup effort.

On one of our most eventful trips, we were traveling to our assigned neighborhood and came to an abrupt stop because there was a house completely intact sitting in the middle of the road. It looked as though someone could actually live in it. Didn't seem like much damage, just not the ideal location. The bus certainly would not be blocking any traffic so the decision was made to leave it there and we would simply ask people in this vicinity if they needed help.

Just by chance, on this particular Saturday, nearly all of our volunteers were black key clubbers; and as we all exited the bus, a woman quickly approached us and asked our intentions. We didn't get the same welcome as Ms. Sally affectionately warmed us with, and it was obvious this woman did not think we were "angels from heaven." We informed her we just wanted to help and asked if she needed any assistance. She was rude and arrogant as she turned away mumbling under her breath. It was evident that she did not trust us, thinking perhaps that we were looters. These folks have been through a lot but we were certainly disappointed in the way we were treated.

Her neighbors were far more hospitable and very much appreciated our help. We giggled as we could see this woman watching from a distance, not letting us out of her sight. We all worked hard, doing all that was asked of us, and as work there was winding down, we began loading up our gear. The woman approached us once again, this time very differently. She was so apologetic; with tears running down her cheeks, she said that she was so sorry for being so judgmental. When we pulled up, she just assumed the worse, assumed people were there to take advantage of her. She said she couldn't fathom that young black teens would travel so far to help strangers and expecting absolutely nothing in return. She gave each one of us a hug and thanked us for what we were doing.

We were all blessed by what had just transpired, and I believe we all had a better appreciation for each other because too often each of us could be accused of judging another falsely, because we judge prematurely. We learned, too, it's a blessing to be the "forgiver" as well as the "forgiven."

Obviously, I am only able to highlight portions of this particular project, but to clarify the magnitude of the accumulated service hours, donations raised, number of members involved, this service project was submitted at the annual Key Club convention and won top honors on the district level and then went on to win First Place at the international convention. Key Club has approximately 5,000 clubs and is in thirty countries. Pretty amazing!

This is just one of a multitude of club projects in which this group was involved. In a span of twenty-two years, key clubbers from this one small high school had logged in over 130,000 community service hours and had raised nearly $300,000 for many, many charitable organizations through the dedication of 1,500 members and had won top honors at the international convention a dozen times.

Key Club's motto is "Caring...Our Way of Life." I believe that you just witnessed that first hand in these past few pages.

Kids these days!

"Truly I say to you, to the extent that you did it to one of these brothers of mine, even the least of them, you did it to Me."
(Matthew 25:40 NASB)

Beyond Appearance

When our school district increased the high school graduation requirements to twenty-four credits, it created quite a stir. I wasn't sure what the problem was. Most schools were on a six-period schedule. Four years, six credits per year, twenty-four credits at the end of the senior year. Simple math, this should work. However, things came to a screeching halt! This was not acceptable! It didn't allow for failure! Something had to be done for students who were going to fail classes. So, as what happens too often in our education system, we made plans for failure rather than ensure success. The solution was to shorten all class periods and have a seven-period day. Shorten class periods where time was already a rare commodity when attempting to teach all standards mandated by the state. Seven-period schedule created another problem—additional classes needed to be taught for the majority of students who were going to inevitably acquire twenty-eight credits.

The principal challenged the faculty to not just come up with fresh ideas but be willing to implement them as well. My idea was to have a service-learning class. It would simply be an enhancement of the many things we were already doing through Key Club but allow the students to take on a much more active part in decision making and organizing all the events. Rather than a club that met once a week, a core of the club members would be involved with the planning every day. The principal helped me create the guidelines and curriculum for the class, and it was soon board-approved for the following year.

I had the privilege of teaching this class for nine years before moving on to teach in another school district. These classes were the most diverse group of students you could possibly find in any classroom setting. It was not unusual to have the valedictorian working side by side with those struggling to just get by. There would be students who were excited about the community service aspect and others who just thought this would be an easy credit. There were always those who strived to make a difference and those who strived to make excuses. They were a typical cross section of today's society—the givers and the takers. I made it a personal challenge to change the hearts and minds of those whom I perceived to be on track to be a burden on our society in their adulthood.

Each new school year brought in a new group and always new challenges. I spotted him on the first day—saggy britches, shoulder length dreads. As he walked into the room, he headed straight to the back and there he took up residence. He didn't seem to share my enthusiasm for the upcoming year with the many ideas and possibilities I had laid out before them. I wasn't certain if he was even awake, wondering why students like that even sign up for a class like this. I dealt with them in the past and was thinking of how I was going to deal with this one.

As the school year progressed, the students began multiple activities, all which took them outside. Day after day, Twon refused to join any group. I confronted him saying that his grade would strongly reflect his participation, which at this point was *zero*. His response was that it was just too hot to go outside. He needed an inside job. Then he questioned me, referring to my statements from the first day of school, "What about this nursing home thing that you mentioned. What can we do there?" I turned it right back on him with a challenge. "You go to the nursing home, you talk to the director, and you come back and tell the group what we can do there." We were no strangers to this particular home, the school was only a couple of miles from them, and Key Clubs of past years have developed a wonderful relationship with the administration and the residents. We would visit and have parties for them on various occasions.

The following day, Twon did indeed go to the home and chatted with the director. He reported that they were fine if we just go hang out with them for a while, and that is what he did. To keep from sweating outside, he chose to visit those residents every day. I believe what he didn't count on was becoming so attached to them. The director of the home soon called me and told me that the gentlemen there loved this young man. Twon would check in with me each day before heading to the home sharing his experiences of the previous day. He spoke of playing checkers with Mr. Charles and his excitement when he finally was able to win a game. He spoke of the stories told of days gone by that the residents were eager to share. He spoke affectionately of Ms. Ruby and how sweet she was. Each day he shared new stories, and his excitement was contagious. Twon broke many barriers as he developed these relationships—those of race, gender, age, socioeconomic…His new friends didn't see color, saggy pants, long dreads—just a young man who cared enough to share a little time to help fill their long empty days.

Each year the county fair rolls into town near the end of October and on one pre-selected afternoon those running the fair open their gates only to the elderly and special needs people free of charge. The director of the nursing home always asks that I send students to the fair to take their residents around on the rides and simply be their buddy for the day.

With much anticipation, from young and old, the big day finally arrived. Teaching responsibilities kept me from attending this event, but it was so evident that all who participated had a wonderful time. The many pictures that were taken were verification of this claim.

Libby, a recent graduate and past key clubber came home from college to participate in this event. She shared with me that Twon had won an extremely large stuffed animal when playing one of the games. He was so excited and told all of us that he was going to give it to his girlfriend when he got home. While he was boastfully carrying this overstuffed creature around, he couldn't help but notice that one of the residents from the home kept eyeing his prize. She looked at it with amazement; she refused to take her eyes off of it. Twon could stand it no longer, and offered his girlfriend's gift to this little lady. Her excitement about receiving this gift was only exceeded by Libby's. Libby explained that as she watched this scene unfold, tears filled her eyes. She then approached Twon with a hug saying, "I'm so proud of you!" "You are so amazing!"

When asking Twon about these events at a later date, he explained that he just had to give that stuffed animal to that lady. It was as though he had no choice. However, what he didn't expect was Libby's response and how wonderful it made him feel. Twon said that he didn't believe that he had ever given away something that he really wanted to someone else without any expectation of anything in return. He went on to say, that after doing so, he experienced a happiness that he would never forget.

One day Twon regretted his words as soon as he spoke them. As a friend of mine likes to say, Words are like toothpaste from its tube, once out there is no putting it back. He told me that he needed to leave quickly so he could buy cigarettes for some of the guys at the home. "Oops! I didn't mean to share that with you." After my coercing, he went on to tell me that he would take cigarettes and mints to them on a regular basis. I was confident that Twon would have no problem getting the cigarettes even at his young age; my concern was that these men where taking advantage of Twon's hospitality.

I knew that he went right on to work after leaving the nursing home and worked late most nights at the Pizza Hut. He, along with other siblings, lived with his grandmother, and he worked to help supplement her meager income. When I questioned Twon about this, he laughed and said, "They can't take advantage of me when this is something that I want to do." I asked about the money. He quickly slapped both hands down onto the front of his jeans. "When I cash my paycheck, the money I need for expenses goes in this pocket; the money I have extra goes into the other, and that's what I use for them," he stated so matter-of-factly. That beautiful face lined with those long dreads and an amazing grin that showed off his two shiny gold front teeth continued to capture my heart. My initial opinion of this young man had already undergone a major transformation, but the things that he did never ceased to amaze me.

Twon wasn't very interested in the holiday parties that this class organized. Due to his work schedule, he wasn't able to attend them anyway. He was the day-to-day guy and turned the event planning over to the others. However, in early December, he approached the class with the idea of getting Christmas gifts for each of the residents at the home. He was questioned as to what kind of gift would be appropriate. He simply said, "We need to give them something that helps them feel good about themselves." My immediate thought was that he has been doing that for them every day. When the students needed something more concrete, he suggested lotions, colognes, shaving-gel, shampoo... At the Christmas party that Twon was unable to attend, each of the nearly fifty residents received a Christmas stocking filled with numerous personal hygiene items and lots of candy. The stockings were handed out by Santa himself; and the residents' excitement mirrored that of small children on Christmas morning. That evening everyone felt a little better about themselves.

When the school year was well underway, the principal approached me stating that he was very much interested in starting a peer mediation program at our school and was in hopes of using my service learning students to implement this program. I was thrilled with this opportunity because I had heard of great successes that another school in our county had, who had employed this program. In fact, the students at that school would actually be the ones training my kids.

The program was designed for students to deal with much of the minor discipline issues at school; things like the constant teenage drama, he-said-she-said kind of "stuff." We would be handling petty things that often disrupt classrooms and consume too much of the administration's time. My students spent many hours going through a training program so that they could be mediators in various situations. During the training process, my students had many opportunities to open up about a variety of personal situations that they have encountered.

I remember when the topic of prejudices was being discussed. It wasn't just about black and white; it was much more than that. Every one of the students admitted to judging others by the way they looked, be it tattoos, purple hair, body piercings... Twon shared that people prejudge him constantly because of his clothes and hair. He told us stories that the resource officer at school would always come looking for him if there was a problem and he had been remotely close to the crime scene. The officer warned Twon, "I've got my eye on you." He said the same was true with the administration—he was always guilty until he could prove his innocence. He said even going into Walmart, it didn't take long for security to start following him around. He admitted that sometimes, just for fun, he would wear a long coat into that store to see how long before he heard, "We need security in aisle number...!"

His revelation caused me to reflect back on that first day he walked into my classroom. Mentally, I had done the very same thing. I was very judgmental of Twon before having an opportunity to get to know him. It seems as though I was not the only one, as we all began to apologize. Many students, both mine and our guests', admitted to judging others within the group. There was more forgiveness flowing late that afternoon than in any church revival.

Twon proved to be a natural when it came to mediating many situations that we encountered. He was street smart and well trained in this process. His peers looked up to him and respected what he had to say. Twon had little trouble getting the opposing parties reconciled. He was a wonderful asset to this program.

Twon was a surprisingly good young man. His home life offered him many opportunities to make wrong decisions, as many of his family members had done. His grandmother rescued him and his siblings and was doing the best she could, but ultimately everyone makes their own choices and must be responsible for them. Grandmother's influence wasn't always enough to keep family out of trouble. However, I never heard of Twon getting into any altercations in school or out.

It seems that in most any setting where there is a group of people, someone stands out as the "favorite." Many are special, but only one is the favorite. Ms. Ruby was that person at the nursing home. For several years, my kids would visit the home, and everyone, me included, was drawn to Ms. Ruby. She was the first we would say hello to and the last one to get our good-byes. For some, she would be the only reason they would visit the home. If she knew we were coming, she would wait in the rocker on the front porch. She was like family.

It was a Sunday morning, I was reading the newspaper, and for some reason I was drawn to the obituary section. I couldn't believe my eyes. It was Ms. Ruby! Sure she had been sick, in and out of the hospital several times. We had visited her there and she had been released to go back to the nursing home. This must be someone else. I called the home and chatted with the director. She confirmed what I already knew but was unwilling to accept.

Her viewing was that afternoon. I immediately got on

the phone and started calling my kids. I tried every number that I knew to try in an attempt to reach Twon, but each attempt was in vain. About twenty students past and present met me at the funeral home for the viewing. One of the girls drove about fifty miles from the college she was attending to be with us. Ms. Ruby's family was overwhelmed to see us. They shared that their mom loved us so much, that we were all she ever wanted to talk about. The owner of the home implored us to continue our work at the nursing home and reminded us that there were so many who still needed us.

We prayed together and then we went to Ryan's Steakhouse and ate together and shared Ms. Ruby stories the rest of the evening.

The next day, when Twon came into class, he said that his grandmother told him that I was trying to get in touch with him yesterday and was wondering what was up. When I told him that Ms. Ruby had passed away, he went to his seat. In spite of his attempt to remain strong, tears rolled down his cheeks as he muttered, "Now that is just wrong. That is so wrong."

Spring break had come and gone way too fast. It was time to head back to school and focus on completing the school year. As the students were entering the classroom, a young man whom I did not recognize entered, or did I? Oh my gosh! It was Twon! I knew he was heading to Florida to see his mom, what I didn't know was that when he returned he would ask his girlfriend to cut his hair. He carried a large brown paper bag; and when I inquired about the contents he showed me his dreads, I guess he wasn't quite ready to part with them.

He stayed after class to share with me about many decisions he was contemplating. He stated that he did not need the hair anymore. He said there was a time when the hair and clothes made a statement about him but he was no longer that person. He said he was different and that he was proud of the person that he had become. One of his regrets was that his gold teeth were permanent and that he would get rid of those if he could. He told me that he was talking to a recruiter and that he was considering joining the marines. I countered that the marines are the toughest of all the military options, and he stated that he felt that he needed the discipline they had to offer.

As the school year was winding down, everyone was excited about graduation and the upcoming break. Twon was working out, running sprints and distance, always attempting to cut seconds off his mile run. He was focused, he had a purpose, he was committed. He wanted to excel in this endeavor. He wanted to be a marine.

Twon did join the marines, and he was a fine recruit. It wasn't long after he finished his initial training that this young man who found it too hot to do our projects on campus was in the heat of war in Afghanistan. Almost exactly one year after I said good-bye to him, he walks into my classroom with the biggest grin and a hug to match. He was so handsome in his uniform and he wore it proudly. He shared stories that made me want to cry and others where we laughed uncontrollably. I was thrilled to spend time once again with this amazing young man, this American hero. After Twon left my room, I thought what a privilege it had been to witness his transformation from a boy into a magnificent young man.

I contacted each person in every chapter, to share my endeavor to write this book. I wanted them to read and validate all that had been written about them and to ensure that my memories of the past coincided with theirs. When I did an online search for Twon the screen read "1 Twon Hickson in the U S" I just smiled because I already knew that this young man was one of a kind.

Kids these days!

"Do you not know that those who run in a race all run, but only one receives the prize? Run in such a way that you may win."

(Corinthians 9:24 NASB)

Champion for the Underdog

Matt was a handsome young man, quite the athlete, played on the state championship football team, a little cocky, a good student who was just an all-around good guy. It seemed that everyone liked him. He had a great personality and always had something nice to say to make you feel a little bit better. Matt had an amazing positive attitude, always upbeat, always wore a smile.

As a senior, Matt was in my service-learning class. This was an elective class in which students developed programs that were of service to the school as well as the community. This group of young people would brainstorm numerous ideas, and I challenged these students to transform these ideas into reality. This was a totally new concept for them. They had been used to sitting in a class where the teacher dictated what was to be done. They were thrilled with the opportunity to create their own course syllabus. The class size dictated the need for numerous and continuous projects to keep these students engaged throughout the class time and throughout the school year.

Projects varied from year to year as interests of new students and needs of the school as well as the community changed. Projects, just to name a few, included such activities as the school newspaper, landscaping on campus, assisting with the special needs class, building and maintaining a one-mile trail in the woods on our campus that was used by various classes for numerous reasons, picking up trash on campus, washing teachers' cars as a fund-raiser... In addition, there were activities that took students away from campus such as tutoring at the feeder schools, visiting a local nursing home two miles from the school, tutoring at a home for abused children, and planning numerous parties that we would have in the evening at both of these homes.

No student worked alone. I encouraged students to work in small groups of two or three. Groups were not assigned; it seemed things worked better when students were allowed to work with peers of their own choosing.

At the beginning of the year, as students were heading out for the first time, it was interesting to see how they paired up—the girls were to work with another girl, and guys the same, for obvious reasons. Everyone naturally hooked up with one of their friends. But as these small groups were forming, I saw something pretty incredible take place. Many of the guys approached Matt asking him to be their partner. Denying the requests of his friends, he approached the desk of a young man who suffered from cerebral palsy. This illness couldn't be hidden because of its crippling effect on its young victim. Matt patted him on the shoulder and said, "Come on, beloved, I want you to be my partner." And partners they were for the entire school year. That was probably the first time anyone had ever chosen him to be on their team. The name of the young man escapes me, but I'll never forget Matt's name for him. "Beloved" was so proud to walk step-in-step with Matt. I was amazed as I witnessed so much compassion from someone so young.

In the spring of that year, one of my students–lost her battle with a lifelong illness. I had become very close to this young lady, and the realization that she was gone was a difficult concept to grasp. She had passed away on a Sunday, which made starting this new workweek nearly inconceivable. As my alarm sounded, I was so tempted to call in sick and simply roll back over putting all my emotions on hold, at least temporarily. I just wasn't ready to deal with the reality of this loss. Then I realized that there would be many students at school feeling the same way. I needed to be there for her friends who were also suffering from the passing of this amazing young lady.

Sitting in my classroom before school began, I attempted to make myself numb to my own emotions in an attempt to at least be a physical presence for those needing to talk about their pain, and to share their loss. I was heading to the office to sign in and check my mailbox when I encountered Matt, who was just entering the school. I was shocked to see him for I knew he was a longtime friend of this young lady, and he would be heartbroken.

As he approached me, I told him that I was shocked to see him at school. He seemingly ignored my comment and asked sincerely how I was doing. I couldn't respond for fear that sharing my feelings would stir emotions that would render me useless, incapable of doing the job that I had envisioned was mine for this difficult day. I simply shrugged my shoulders, unable to speak. With a hug, he spoke, "I want you to know that she loved you so much." That statement made it impossible for me to control the tears.

Matt wouldn't stay home because he was thinking as I—many would be hurting and would need comforting. I'm so glad he was there for me that morning; it made my task a little easier. Once again I was amazed at his compassion and his willingness to put the needs of others above his own.

About two months later, the school year was drawing to a close, and no one was more excited about the year's end than the seniors (except maybe the teachers). Many activities had been put into place throughout the years to celebrate this group's accomplishment. Graduation!

One of the most coveted of all privileges was Field Day—a full day of fun, competitive activities where senior homerooms came head-to-head to determine which group would reign supreme. At least a month prior to this event, the students would begin discussing and voting on their team name and color of their T-shirts that they would wear into battle.

Eventually, the big day arrived. Competitions throughout the morning were held in the gymnasium—events such as volleyball, basketball, free throw and hula hoop contests. While the students were inside, parents and alumni were on the football field grilling burgers and hotdogs for lunch. After lunch, the games continued—games more suited for the outdoors like football and softball throws, egg and water balloon toss, tricycle relay, and tug-a-war to name a few.

Everyone was having a great time. Some students chose to sit back and enjoy time with friends and simply cheer on their team. Others had a more competitive spirit and preferred to participate in everything they could. Everyone wanted the bragging rights of being the victors of Field Day! The excitement mounted throughout the afternoon as point totals were announced periodically.

There was a special group of seniors who were not in homerooms with the rest of the student body. This group of students was mentally challenged and required special attention from their teachers and aides. Each year, one of the aides would purchase T-shirts for these amazing teenagers, and I would have them wear my homeroom's shirt so that they were a part of our team. These children rarely wanted to compete, but if they did, they were on the egg or water balloon toss, or something that didn't require much "expertise." They were thrilled because everyone who wanted to do something did.

As typically happens, the softball tournament—the final competition of the day—would determine who would reign victorious. The teachers were every bit as competitive as the students. We were the biggest cheerleaders because our bragging rights lasted long after these seniors graduated.

It was the bottom of the last inning in the championship game. This win would give my team the points we needed to win Field Day. The tying run was on first base. I pulled the batting order card from pocket, searching to see who was up next. I was thrilled to see Matt step up to the plate. The outfield all began to back up, anticipating the inevitable. I felt the game was in the proverbial bag.

I was confused as Matt stepped away from the plate and walked past me. I questioned what he was doing. There was Timmy (not his name) from the special needs class with our team shirt on, watching the game with such excitement. While handing him the bat, Matt asked if he wanted to play. Timmy was so excited as he snatched the bat and ran to the plate. Everything inside of me screamed, "Noooo!" The team raced to Matt, questioning, "What are you doing?" He reminded us, "It's just a game and I could tell he really wanted to play."

I didn't even notice Timmy standing close by, all I was focused on was winning, but Matt saw a young man who, for a few minutes, wanted to be like everyone else.

When Timmy stepped up to the plate, the opposing team all stepped in much closer. Timmy surprised us all by actually hitting the ball. The ball didn't go very far, but he had the whole infield scrambling as they realized he was going to make it to first base. To everyone's surprise, Timmy kept running! The infield, in desperation, overthrew second base, and Timmy kept running as his teammates screamed for him to stop.

Finally Matt ran on the field, grabbed Timmy at third base, and physically persuaded him to stop. The next batter's hit allowed Timmy to score the game-winning run.

I really feel like God blessed Matt's decision to allow Timmy to bat in his place. Had Timmy struck out, I believe most everyone on the team would have resented him. Matt really had a lot riding on his very thoughtful gesture. Matt knew with one swing of the bat, he could have been the hero of our team. Peer pressure would not have allowed most of us to be so thoughtful, so generous. He took a chance; he stepped up and did what was on his heart, and God blessed both of them for his courageous decision. This was a World Series win for Timmy, and as far as I'm concerned, Matt was the hero of our team.

Matt went on to graduate high school a few weeks later. He attended college locally, which enabled him to assist with the coaching of the varsity and JV football teams at his alma mater. He remained very much involved with activities on this campus, always willing to step up when called upon. Several years later, with his degree in hand, he returned to this campus assisting with the special needs students and shortly after became the career counselor. He continues coaching sports, and now with his new assignment, he is coaching students into future career paths as well. As a champion for the underdog, he continues changing the lives of young people, convincing them they have a purpose in life and guiding them on a path to success.

Kids these days!

"In everything, therefore, treat people the
same way you want them to treat you."
(Matthew 7:12 NASB)

Strangers; Friends We Have Yet to Meet

For two days, the textbooks remained unopened as we turned our attention to the television. For two days we were mesmerized with the events unfolding as we watched in horror the terror attacks on our great country. In a futile attempt to hold back the tears, we helplessly witnessed the pain, the suffering, the devastation. It was a horrific day that has simply become known as "9/11."

Group after group filed into my classroom as the day progressed, each class asking the same questions; the same questions that the entire world was asking. "Why?" "How could anyone want to do this to us?" It is one thing to attack our military, but the thousands of innocents? This we could not comprehend.

It didn't take long for Key Club and service learning students to begin asking what they could do. They felt doing something would somehow help ease the pain and helplessness we all felt.

As we brainstormed ideas, many suggested ways to raise money to donate to Red Cross or United Way and allow those organizations to use the money as they thought best. Others didn't like the idea of turning the money over to such large groups, because we would never know how our donations would be used. Many students wanted to have a greater say in the distribution of funds, just wasn't sure what, where, and how.

Brad was the most boisterous of the group in his disapproval of turning over the money from any of our fundraising efforts to another organization. I in turn challenged him to come up with a better idea. Brad was just a regular guy and, like most teenage boys, much preferred sports to academics. However, Brad might have been a little more mischievous than most. It's really not a good thing when the assistant principal knows your home phone number by heart. I'm still convinced that he played a major part in the release of a wild pig in the school hallway, early one morning, near the end of his senior year. I do wish, though, that I could've seen school personnel chasing after that squealing pig through the hallways.

Once again the topic of 9/11 came up the following day during service-learning class, and Brad stated simply that we just need to find a family of our own and work with them. He wanted to adopt a family of a fallen firefighter. I'm certain that being the son of a volunteer firefighter and a volunteer fireman himself is what swayed him in this direction. I told Brad that I would find a family, and he needed to begin organizing fundraising efforts. Brad quickly became totally absorbed with his responsibilities.

Because of the many press releases of our numerous projects throughout the years, I had become well acquainted with one of the local newspaper reporters. I called Bill and shared with him our desire to find a 9/11 family and my ignorance as to how to pursue this quest. I explained my reasoning in soliciting his help. I figured because he was a newspaper reporter, he would have connections with newspaper reporters everywhere and could assist us in finding our family. He assured me it didn't work just like that, but he would be delighted to engage in this endeavor.

He shared with me that on that very evening, as he sat at his computer with the list of fallen firefighters on his screen, he began to pray. He asked God to share with him the name of the family that we were to adopt. His prayer was answered. "So the last shall be first," (Matthew 20:16 NASB) He scrolled to the bottom of the list and found the name Raymond York. Raymond York's family immediately became our family. He called the precinct where Ray had worked and talked with Captain Don and shared with him our group's intentions.

I called Captain Don, and he shared my enthusiasm in working with the York family. He gave us the names and ages of Ray's four children. However, he cautioned me that Ray's wife, Joan, was absolutely devastated and not to be surprised if she did not immediately respond to our endeavor. That was perfectly understandable, and we were not looking for recognition. We simply wanted them to know that people 800 miles away cared about them; cared about their loss.

Brad had recruited the assistance of a couple of the girls in the service-learning class, and together they designed a very patriotic T-shirt with our school logo filled with the stars and stripes of the American flag. We ordered hundreds of those shirts, and for a couple of months we were in the T-shirt business. The shirts were a big hit; teachers and students alike were proud to wear a shirt that displayed pride in school and country. The high school football games provided a wonderful venue for this incredible undertaking. It was Brad who patrolled the parking lots searching for customers to purchase this merchandise. The shirts sold very quickly for several weeks as we continued buying additional shirts to sell. As time passed, it became more difficult to move these items, but Brad was unrelenting in his mission. With about twenty shirts remaining, Brad went to our state championship football game with shirts in his backpack, selling them to strangers. He sold them all, later laughing about even selling our school shirts to the fans of our opponents whom we had just defeated by one point. He said that they liked the design and wanted it mostly because of its patriotic look.

This venture wasn't only about raising money. We realized that the victims would eventually be getting money from this horrendous event, but we also knew those things take time, and we wanted to assist in the transitional time especially with the holidays quickly approaching.

Students organized and assisted with a very successful blood drive in memory of Raymond York. This blood drive has become an annual event. Each year, on or around 9/11, a blood drive is held at the high school in Ray's memory. On each drive, approximately one hundred pints of blood are donated. Even though the drive is open to the community, almost all of the donors are the students themselves.

Students wanted to share a little bit of themselves with our new family. Items began coming in. It seemed only natural that each one in the York family would receive a Key Club T-shirt and the T-shirts that netted $8,000 from our fundraiser, but then most of our school's clubs and sports team wanted to get involved as well, donating hats and shirts. Some of the local stores in our community also donated items displaying the name of our city or lovely state. We just wanted the York family to have a sense of who we were. But I think the best thing that went into that large box were the scores and scores and scores of letters that were written to each member of the family. Students sharing a little about themselves but more importantly how impressed they were of Ray and what an amazing hero he was.

The students were proud that they took such an active role in this disaster that struck our country, through reaching out to a family whose lives changed in an instant. But shortly after, students began inquiring if I had heard from our family. My answer was always the same, "No response yet." But then I was quick to remind them that we did not do this to receive any accolades;

we just wanted to let them know that we cared about them and what they were going through.

I had stayed in touch with Captain Don and was aware of the fact that Joan was overcome with grief and overwhelmed with raising these children alone. I had resigned myself to believe that I would never hear from her. However, that did not stop us from continuing to reach out to them. In March, six months after that disastrous day, we once again wrote letters to the family. We wanted them to know that we had not forgotten them. Once again, we sent out letters of support, encouragement, and of love. This time was a little different. Approximately one hundred letters were written and each one addressed and stamped individually. I would have loved to have seen the mailman attempting to deliver these letters to this house and then to see the faces of the children as they received so much mail. We all laughed as we envisioned such a scenario.

In early April, I received a phone call from Joan, and I was thrilled beyond belief. She said that she wanted to come to our school and personally thank all these students who were so thoughtful and had reached out to her and her family when they were in such despair. She accepted my invitation to not only attend our annual Spring Key Club Banquet but to be our guest speaker as well.

The students were amazed that Joan was coming, and everyone wanted to ensure that her stay would be perfect. Students had many ideas, and I encouraged each to pursue them. A letter to the editor was written in our local newspaper describing the entire project and the anticipated arrival of our guest. We asked that our "All-America City" (a recognition that our city had recently received) give our guest an all-American welcome. Local businesses and citizens were asked to send something to our guests' hotel room to welcome them to our city. The letter stated that, "More than anything, we want this family to know that they have a family right here that cares about their pain, that appreciates the ultimate sacrifice that Ray York and so many others paid while attempting to save the lives of strangers."

Students followed through as expected. One student had allocated a rental car for Joan to use during her stay. The Holiday Inn Express committed to free lodging. The parents of one of the students offered frequent flier miles, which proved unnecessary. Other students were soliciting souvenir-type donations. Brad inquired about having Joan come by the fire station so she could meet the firefighters there. That idea quickly evolved into a cookout where the entire community was invited.

The big day had arrived. Joan, along with her daughter Kristen, would be flying into an airport nearly an hour away. My daughter and I had the pleasure of picking them up. When we arrived, Laura, a key clubber from the past who was attending college nearby, greeted us. She also invited a local firefighter to join us. In addition, Laura had made a large, colorful sign welcoming our friends to South Carolina.

Joan had no problem spotting us in this small airport. We exchanged hugs and introductions and we were quickly on our way. As we pulled into the parking lot of the hotel, Joan was greeted by a large welcoming committee of key clubbers. Brad was quick to grab suitcases and head to the front desk for check-in. When Joan opened the door of her hotel room, we were all amazed at the numerous gifts and flowers that the community had sent to welcome her.

The next evening was the cookout at the fire station. As we drove up, the ladder truck was out, with the ladder fully extended, and on the ladder waved a huge American flag. The very sight of it brought tears to my eyes. There was a great turnout. Many people were wishing to meet Joan and Kristen. Many had questions but most simply wanted to express their pride in Ray and sympathy for Joan's loss. The newspaper and TV station were at this event interviewing Joan, myself, and club officers, Jayme and Katie who played a major role in this entire project from day one. Brad chose to remain in the background, flipping dogs and burgers on the grill. He wasn't interested in any attention or special recognition. A job well done was reward enough.

The following evening was the long-awaited, greatly anticipated, well-planned-out banquet. Club officers did a magnificent job orchestrating every aspect of this event. As they emceed this affair, they introduced the first guest speaker. Betty Ryberg, wife of our state senator, presented the state flag to Joan. It had flown over the state capitol just a few days prior to this event.

In addition, she gifted Joan with a South Carolina blanket and few instructions. "During those cold New York winters, I want you to wrap this blanket around you and your children and know that the people in South Carolina just gave you a warm hug."

After the meal, Joan York was introduced. Joan began by describing her husband as an exemplary man, an excellent father, with a gift for teaching fire safety to young children. She spoke of the manner in which we selected Ray, "The last shall be first." She shared that due to a shoulder injury, Ray was the last firefighter expected to be on the scene but one of the first to courageously charge in without hesitation into what proved to be a deathtrap on September 11. She went on to say, "Your kindness has meant more than you'll ever know. We've been blessed with so much support from my family, the fire department and my community, but I kind of expected that, because they knew us, and they love us. What I didn't expect was to go to my mailbox one day and have it overflowing with mail from this city. Where is this place? It's a town I'd never heard of, but I know now I'll never forget." She went on to say that she was overwhelmed with the money that was raised and the gifts that were sent, especially the letters.

In reference to the terrorist attack, she stated, "When something like this happens, it's very easy to dwell on the evil, and you helped to remind us that there's so much more good in this world than there is bad." She explained that when her children received that first batch of letters and read them and shared them with each other, they all began laughing and smiling again, and that, she said, was a gift to her.

Joan stated, "A while after that, we received a second mailing, and I remember thinking I have about one hundred angels in South Carolina because I was having a really bad day, and all of a sudden my mailbox was full again, and I thought somebody's watching over me and he's working through those kids in South Carolina." As Joan concluded, the tears flowed from all as we joined in a standing ovation.

That day we honored the family of Raymond York, a firefighter, a martyr for a cause. He, like so many that day, rushed in to save others with no regard for his own safety, or ultimately, his own life. We felt that somehow by honoring Ray York through his wife and children, we honor all those firefighters who put their lives in harm's way every time they jump on that fire truck.

I'm confident that every year when September 11th rolls around, there are about one hundred kids (now adults) who relive the impact of their generosity and remember that life is so much more precious when we reach out and help a stranger, who's not really a stranger after all, just a friend we have yet to meet.

I have been gifted a wonderful friendship with Joan that has withstood the test of time and distance. As for Brad... once again, I was privileged to witness a young mischievous boy put aside his childlike behavior and enter into manhood. Brad's life was forever changed by this moment in history and the way he chose to respond.

Kids these days!

"Give and it shall be given unto you; good measure, pressed down, and shaken together, and running over."

(Luke 6:38 NIV)

Chapter 10

Against the Odds

It was about a week before Christmas. Co-Key Club advisor Dru and I were delivering Christmas gifts to the home of a desperately needy family. Through the encouragement of the school guidance counselor, Key Club was sponsoring this family for Christmas. The dozens of gifts in the brightly colored wrappings were not the typical gifts on children's wish list. No, these were necessities—clothes, shoes, socks, underwear, jackets...

As we pulled off the highway and into the yard, two young brothers ran out to the car barefooted to greet us. Their mom, a relatively young woman but aged beyond her years, stood with her other children where they greeted us at the door. The gifts remained in the car as we entered the home awaiting instructions as to how we were going to keep our Christmas cargo a secret from the children.

I had driven past this structure that they called home many times, never thinking about people actually living within its walls. Many windows were covered with plywood where large shards of windowpane still remained. As we entered the home, I was amazed as I stepped into the front room that through the floorboards,

I could actually see the ground below. There was a wood-burning stove standing in the middle of the home that was used to provide heat for the entire place. Looking into the bedrooms which were dimly lit by the late afternoon sun filtering through large gaps in the plywood, I saw mattresses on the floor and clothes scattered about. I don't think that I have ever witnessed such deplorable living conditions in my life.

This very tiny, overcrowded structure was the home of Troy Williamson. Troy was just a youngster at the time and younger siblings were still to be born. His mom had a total of eleven children, which proved to be far more than she could care for alone. Government assistance was misused, and there never seemed to be a positive male role model in this home. It was through the loving care of their grandmother, who lived behind them, and the generosity of neighbors and church members that this family was able to survive.

I recall that his two older sisters actually moved into the homes of other families where they were cared for. These two young ladies are amazing success stories. They both went to college; one actually graduated from the US Naval Academy. In addition, Troy had an older brother who, upon graduating high school, joined the military. They never used poverty as an excuse; rather, they used their energy, intelligence, and the assistance of others to rise above this poverty stricken, government-dependent lifestyle. All three chose different paths, but all found avenues to escape this destitution.

As those three one by one moved away to pursue their goals, so too did the positive attitude, determination, strong work ethic, belief in God and self also vanished from the home. Those ingredients for success were no longer visible, and they soon faded from memory.

Troy, along with an older brother, chose a different path. They ran the streets all hours of the night. They were mischievous, and trouble seemed to be their constant companion. Their mom had no control over them; her rules, as well as the rules at school, were simply ignored.

On two separate occasions, unsupervised play turned tragic for Troy. Twice Troy was a victim of children playing with fire. The first accident left Troy with third-degree burns on nearly 20 percent of his small body. Skin grafts were taken from one side of his body in an attempt to re-grow skin on the other side. For three months, this nine-year-old boy was bedridden in the hospital in hopes that his fragile body would be restored. When the event happened, he recalled being in so much pain that as he was being rushed to the hospital, his one question, "Am I going to die?"

After the burns healed, Troy was faced with an additional impediment, he had lost all muscle tone in his legs from their lack of use. He literally had to learn to walk again. Rehabilitation was long, painful, and challenging, and Troy learned at a very young age that life was not easy.

It was only a few years later that Troy once again found himself in the burn unit of a local hospital. This time his foot received third-degree burns. The burns were not nearly as severe as the past, but this accident still required skin grafts, a hospital stay, and additional scars, both mental and physical, to be worn for a lifetime as a constant reminder of these tragic incidents.

There was a young man from a local church who offered to assist Troy's mom in the disciplining of Troy and his older brother. She was desperate for help and was quick to take Doug up on his offer. He took them to church with him and attempted to instill in them such traits as character, honor, integrity...He would offer simple rewards for good behavior and obeying curfew hours set by their mom. Troy made a half-hearted attempt to honor his request, but the older brother thought it to be nonsense. It wasn't long before Troy's brother made the headlines of the local paper, "Teen Killed in Crash while Driving a Stolen Vehicle."

After much soul-searching, Troy began to reconsider what his new friend was selling because he witnessed firsthand that the path he was taking was literally a dead-end road. It was about this same time in his life that he discovered that God had blessed him with an incredible talent that he was simply unaware. Running! I'm not certain who discovered it or how it was discovered, but somewhere along the way someone noticed that Troy had incredible speed.

This talent was quickly put to the test in two different sports—track and field along with football. His involvement in church and now in sports provided the perfect structure and discipline this young man needed in his life.

I was privileged to have Troy in my service-learning class and eventually in Key Club. I witnessed firsthand a young man leaving a troubled past and engaging in activities where he was constantly giving to others. Football practice didn't keep Troy from showing up at the children's home for the many parties we would host; he just came a little late. When he did arrive, the young boys would run to greet him and literally hang from his arms and legs. Troy learned quickly that there was so much more pleasure in giving than there was taking.

In preparation for Christmas activities at both the children's home as well as the nursing home, the service-learning class decided to make Christmas stockings for all the residents. My neighbor who worked at the local mill donated all the fabric needed for this endeavor. We found numerous sewing machines in storage at the school and both Jean McElmurray, a past home economics teacher, as well as those sewing machines came out of retirement to make our plan a reality. Jean came to the school numerous times during this class period and patiently taught my students first how to thread the machine and then how to sew. She helped them create patterns for the stockings and the process for putting it all together. We developed an assembly line—some cut out the material, some sewed, others painted the stockings with fabric paint, and still others sought donations of candy and personal hygiene items to place in the stockings. We made and filled 120 stockings that Christmas. I'll never forget witnessing Troy's excitement as he sat at a sewing machine day after day making stockings for our friends.

As for Troy's speed? He proved to be the fastest in the state of South Carolina, where he was a two-time 100- and 200-meter-dash state champion. Troy first put on a high school varsity football jersey as a junior, and the team did not lose a game for the two years that Troy played, which led to back-to-back state championships.

Troy concluded his senior year with multiple titles: All-American, All-State, Class AA Player of the Year, and a Mr. Football finalist, just to name a few. However, Troy was so much more than a football player or someone who could run really fast. He had become a that person of character, compassion, and integrity. The title that Troy had that I was most proud was that of our county's "Youth of the Year," which celebrated all of Troy's newly acquired attributes.

I recall Troy being selected to play for the state's all-star football team in the Shrine Bowl, where the best high school players in South Carolina play against their counterparts of North Carolina. The players miss an entire week of school for practice and preparation for the game. Troy called my cell phone every day he was gone during the service-learning class to see how we were doing. He was so homesick and missed us especially during that time he was normally in this class. We were always anxious to hear from him. He shared when he returned that the best part of the entire week, besides actually playing in the game, was visiting the patients at the Shriners Hospital for Children. He had come a long way from the streets of his childhood.

Troy sat in my classroom the last day of school prior to graduation where we found ourselves chatting about his past and now, amazing opportunities for his future. He had just recently accepted a full scholarship to play football for Lou Holtz, who was coaching the University of South Carolina Gamecocks. He seemed a little nervous about moving forward with his life yet excited about this tremendous opportunity. We talked about all the changes he had made, and I shared with him how proud I was of the man sitting in front of me. He told me that he was so bad in middle school. He stated, "I was bad just to be bad." He went on further, "I remember we were so bad that we caused our teacher to quit. She just couldn't take it anymore, and we found delight in our victory." He said that now it troubled him to think of all the pain that he caused so many. I inquired as to what it was that caused the change in his thinking. He pondered the question for just a moment and said the most important factor was the death of his brother; knowing that if he continued in the same direction, that could easily be his fate as well. I reminded him that he was on the right track now, it was time to move forward, and it was his turn to make a positive difference in the lives of others.

I enjoyed following Troy's college football career. I recall an interview that a sportscaster had with Lou Holtz about his team. Holtz talked of Troy as being one of the most unselfish players he had coached, that Troy took as much delight in being a blocker downfield for another receiver has he did in catching the ball himself. Then he spoke of Troy's compassionate heart when they visited the children's ward at the hospital. Some players had difficulty relating to the children, but not Troy Williamson. Now, he was talking about the Troy that I had come to know and love.

Troy had a great college career and went on to play in the NFL. He was picked up by the Minnesota Vikings in the seventh pick of the first round of the draft. After several years with that franchise, he went on to play for the Jaguars. I recall after signing with the Vikings, Troy decided that he needed a new vehicle. He told me that he went into a new car dealership and was eyeing a Lincoln Navigator on the showroom floor, a car in excess of $60,000. The salesman that was working the floor simply ignored Troy. Others had come and gone and he didn't give Troy the time of day. Troy finally approached the salesman, and the salesman, seemingly annoyed, asked, "May I help you?" Troy responded that he would like for the gentleman to get the manager, or another salesman, because he wished to purchase that new car and he needed assistance. The gentleman quickly and enthusiastically responded that he could help Troy with this purchase. Troy reminded the salesman of his total indifference toward helping him initially and that there was no way he would allow this man to receive any commission or recognition on the purchase of this car. Now I'm certain that Troy was wearing a T-shirt, jeans, sneakers and a ball cap that was precisely tilted at the appropriate angle; and the salesman was thinking that this young black man had no serious business in this establishment. Was he ever mistaken! What do they say? Don't judge a book by its cover. That salesman learned a costly lesson that day.

Prior to the purchase of the car, before his seven-figure check was in the mail, Troy was looking at property and house plans. Not for himself, mind you, it was for his mom. His number one goal, after he went pro, was to take care of his mom. It wasn't long before she moved from a shack to a beautiful four-bedroom, four-bath house in a brand-new subdivision. As for the gentleman from church who rescued Troy from the streets, he now lives in a large home on ten acres of land, compliments of Troy, where he continues to work with young at-risk adolescents. Why ten acres? It is a great place, and a safe place for these young men to ride four-wheelers also provided by Troy.

When Troy was in my service-learning class, he played a very active part in our adoption of the Raymond York family of 9/11. Now as a Viking, I was aware that Troy would be playing the Giants in New York on a Sunday in late October. I spoke to Troy about the possibility of getting tickets for the York family for that game, and Troy made it happen. My daughter, Christy and I flew into New York and spent the weekend with Joan York and her family. Troy made arrangements for us to rendezvous with him at the sports bar of the hotel where they were staying. We were to meet with him after the team meeting the evening before their game. Joan's children were thrilled with the prospect of meeting a NFL player as we anxiously awaited his arrival. Troy came and sat at our table and brought a friend, who just happened to be another previous student of mine, Corey Chavous, who played safety for the Vikings. This was double the excitement. Customers at the establishment came up to these guys asking for photo ops and autographs; Joan's kids whispered among themselves saying, "That's okay, because they are *with* us." After a wonderful visit and an opportunity to catch up, Troy gave us tickets for the Sunday game. We took numerous pictures, and Troy made an extra effort to find me at the high school on Monday after their win against the Giants and autograph those pictures so the kids could have them in a timely fashion. I believe we all felt that the personal time we spent at the sports bar with Troy and Corey was far more exciting than the game itself, and the pictures they received later will keep the memories alive forever.

Troy spent six years in the NFL, and I know that those years were not as memorable as he would have liked, but he did accomplish a dream that only 1 percent of high school players ever achieve. That dream merely catapulted him into his next major dream—helping troubled kids, preferably middle-school children. He wanted to focus on that same age that he was when he was too easily influenced to go astray. He also aspired to take this dream back home, to the same streets, the same neighborhood, where the same temptations that he struggled against were still so prevalent.

Troy Williamson is the founder of Fighting Against the O.D.D.S. Foundation. The mission is to provide diverse opportunities and exposure for young people facing adversity through service learning, scholarship, and physical activity. He is excited about the future and ready to serve. His next big endeavor is to build a sports academy in the community where he grew up.

Troy also is a motivational speaker. He is quick to say that he has been blessed with a story to tell, where he reminds his audience that hardships are a part of life, and learning to deal with them makes you stronger and prepares you for what lies ahead.

After joining the Vikings, Troy married his childhood sweetheart, and their family has continued to grow. The couple now has three handsome sons. Troy says that he is thankful for every blessing bestowed upon him and his goal is to be a blessing to others.

Kids these days!

> "Well done, good and faithful servant.
> You have been faithful over a few things;
> I will put you in charge of many things."
> (Matthew 25:23 NIV)

Seeing Through the Darkness

"Good things come in small packages." It's a proverb that we've all heard and certainly rings true in this situation. As a freshman in my algebra class, Emily Zimmermann did not stand five feet tall, but in my eyes she soon became a giant among her peers.

Emily's last name doomed her to be in the back of my classroom as I typed the seating chart prior to the first day of school. This chart was used for organizational purposes initially, and students were moved about later for discipline and instructional needs. Emily fell into neither category; her grades were great, her demeanor was even better; she was simply destined to be in the back. Because of her small stature, I asked her often if she could see the board, if she was okay with seating arrangements. She always assured me that her seat was just fine.

Typically, the day prior to a test would be spent reviewing. It never failed; there were several boys who always insisted on Emily being in their small study group. After one of these study sessions, Emily shared with me that she had aspirations of being a teacher, she just wasn't sure if she had the patience needed. I assured her that not all students were as distracted as those young promising athletes in her group whose mind was on everything but tomorrow's test.

The months rolled by quickly and the semester was soon drawing to a close when it was discovered that the annoying problems that Emily was experiencing with her sight was caused by a brain tumor, craniopharyngioma, to be exact. Surgery was scheduled immediately to remove this tumor. The removal of this growth did not come without tremendous complications, which followed. Pituitary gland, thyroid gland, sense of smell, short-term memory; all were comprised in a major way and created tremendous imbalances in Emily's body which necessitated numerous visits to the emergency room as well as additional stays in the hospital, as doctors desperately began to sort out all the effects of the damage that was done. In addition to that, a later MRI revealed a piece of the tumor still remaining, which required surgery on her brain once again to remove the fragment. Recuperation was long and difficult.

As Emily was able, the school provided homebound teaching in an attempt to keep her caught up with her classes. A family friend, who was a teacher at the school, was quick to volunteer for this assignment. However, she asked that I assist with the teaching of Algebra, which I felt privileged to do.

I saw firsthand the impact of the memory loss. When we first began the lessons, Emily often wasn't certain of the day of the week or even what she had for lunch that day; this certainly made it difficult to teach anything new. But, through time and determination, her memory began to improve so she was able to progress through the required material that needed to be covered. Due to her health and memory issues, Emily remained on homebound instruction through the remainder of the school year. She completed this course by the end of the school term. However, her other teacher worked with her diligently throughout the summer to complete the rest of her courses. By summer's end, Emily was ready to return to school.

It was early August, and students and teachers alike felt the excitement of starting a new school year. Emily's friends were excited to see her at school once again, and she was thrilled to be there. It wasn't long before Emily's short-term memory was once again a problem. She had trouble remembering her schedule, where certain classes were, where her locker was and the combination. In addition, she was once again faced with eyesight problems. These issues prompted another MRI which revealed her greatest fear; the tumor had indeed grown back.

Early September, Emily was once again being prepped for surgery, once again facing that tremendous trauma to the brain, aware of the long recovery time, aware of the many what-ifs that could possibly happen. Back at school we were *all* in prayer mode, watching the clock, knowing when the surgery was scheduled to occur and anxiously awaiting the results.

The results! The surgery to remove this tumor left

Emily totally blind, complete darkness. The surgeon went back into Emily's skull a couple of days later in hopes of being able to correct the blindness, but it was to no avail. The damage was permanent. Emily was to live her life in darkness.

Emily's mom, Janet, shared with me that shortly after this surgery, the family had gathered in Emily's hospital room, and Emily cheerfully proclaimed, "Isn't God good?" Janet responded in agreement but questioned what prompted the remark, especially due to her current situation. Emily simply said, "It's just amazing how well I can hear." And this is how Emily approached her newly acquired disability, not focused on what she had lost; rather, thanking God for what she had.

Now I'm not going to pretend that Emily did not struggle with the devastating fact that she could no longer see. No! Her world was suddenly turned upside down, and she certainly grieved her loss. Each day brought on new challenges and additional reminders of her newly acquired inadequacies. She couldn't see, but she never lost sight of the fact that God was her strength, her constant companion, and he would walk with her on this new incredibly difficult journey.

I was proud to go forward with Emily on this new journey, as we once again began the homebound instruction at her kitchen table. We were both challenged as I tried to think of creative ways to teach Emily geometry. I laid Twizzlers on a cookie sheet to explain parallel lines being cut by a transversal and the angles that were formed, and when we completed the lesson we proceeded to eat her homework. As I sat at that table day after day, I was blown away by the amazing attitude that this young lady had. In conversation, I often forgot that she was even blind as I told her to look at this or read that. We just laughed, and she said that she was encouraged by the fact that I did not look at her as being blind; rather, I still saw her for who she was. My visits were often lengthened by our many conversations that had nothing to do with school.

She shared that when the last tumor was removed, she not only lost her sight, she also lost her friends as well. I questioned her, because her best friend would come regularly with news of Emily for all to hear; but I quickly found out that this friend, who only lived a few blocks away, never visited, nor were there even phone calls from friends at school. When I returned to school and questioned many, they were full of empty promises to visit or call. I'm not certain what happened, but her so-called friends seemed very intimidated about continuing a relationship with a blind person. Emily said that she would love to talk to her classmates and inform them that she was still the same person, she just couldn't see. The more time I spent with Emily, I discovered that her vision of life far surpassed that of many; it was her friends who were truly blind.

Emily shared, too, that she had been homeschooled through the eighth grade and was very apprehensive about attending high school; even though this school was small by comparison, it was nonetheless very intimidating. She told me that prior to starting school, she prayed, asking God to use her, to help bring others closer to him. She quickly followed that statement, laughingly saying, "Be careful what you pray for," and that she has reminded God periodically that she would certainly be willing to do this task as a sighted disciple.

I thought about Emily's request to speak to her classmates and how I could possibly arrange such a meeting, and then it occurred to me that I could have her speak at the annual Christmas assembly that the Key Club hosted. The entire student body would be present, and she could enlighten the total assembly of her journey thus far and about her intentions of returning to school after the Christmas break. She would have nearly a month to prepare her message.

Well, Emily was scared to death of the thought of speaking before the entire assembly. She questioned how many would be in attendance, and I countered, "What would it matter, you can't see them anyway. Just pretend there are just a few people." She had trouble with my logic and doubts about her ability to pull this off. I informed her that her story would be told at the Christmas assembly. If she didn't do it, that I would, and shared that it would be so much nicer coming from her. Emily had very legitimate concerns about telling her story. Her short-term memory was very much an issue, and reading notes was no longer an option.

Her mom was very much on board with Emily speaking to these students. She saw firsthand the pain that Emily endured with the abandonment of friendships and certainly felt the need to inform these people that Emily was still indeed Emily. Janet continued to encourage Emily to pursue this quest and assisted Emily in how it could be possible.

I had to disagree with Janet; her daughter was not the same person. Emily's life had changed drastically and the way she had chosen to deal with this challenge had matured her far beyond that of her peers. Emily's positive demeanor and constant smile that often broke out into laughter was unimaginable for someone who had so recently experienced such a life-altering event. Not only was Emily a different person, I know that I am a better person for my association with this young lady. She had so quickly put life into an amazing new perspective for me. Often, before the lesson, I would encourage Emily to walk with me in her neighborhood. I always felt that the physical exercise as well as the outdoors would be good for her, and walking blindly was a new experience that needed to be practiced. During one of our walks I asked her about her incredibly positive attitude. She proclaimed that after becoming blind, there were so many things that she could no longer do; so many things that were simply out of her control. However, one of the things she did have control over was her choice of attitude. She said, "I could choose to be depressed and feel sorry for myself, or I could choose to be happy and continue to live my life the best I can. Either way, I'm still going to be blind. So I choose to be happy." She smiled, stating, "Life is so much more enjoyable this way."

Many, many times, I left Emily's home wondering, "Who is the student and who is the teacher?" In my heart, I already knew the answer to that question. Often as I would drive away from the Zimmermanns' home, I would find myself in prayer, thanking God that He allowed me to be a part of Emily's incredible new journey.

The night before the Christmas assembly, my cell phone rang after I had already gone to bed. Answering it, I heard the faint whisper of a young voice saying, "I'll do it." Her decision came late, and I could hear in her voice how hard it was to say yes, but I was thrilled beyond belief that she did.

The Christmas assembly is always a wonderful event held on the final day before the two-week break. The key club collaborates with the entire student body working within their fourth-period class to fill the wish lists of the children at a local home for the abused and neglected. Typically, they service about fifty children during this time of year, and our students do a remarkable job providing Christmas gifts for these youngsters. The student body also has a massive canned food drive sponsored by the youth in the JROTC program, and the band and chorus play and sing Christmas favorites. This year we were privileged to add one more item to the program—the return of Emily Zimmermann to school.

Emily and Janet did a remarkable job telling Emily's story. Emily could not use notes, but her mom provided all the help she needed. Emily began telling her story;

and where her memory faltered, Janet stepped in momentarily and then turned it back over to Emily. It was well rehearsed and the two spoke as one. You could not tell for an instant that either was nervous. They spoke with confidence and they spoke with compassion as Emily's story came to life. Some of the students had no idea prior to this, who Emily even was. Emily had only been able to attend school one semester to this point in her high school endeavor.

As Emily's story unfolded, the tears began to flow. Everyone in the gymnasium was visibly touched about what she had experienced. Emily and Janet were sharing a story that was just in its infancy. This was just the beginning. As they concluded, Emily received a standing ovation; and as the program came to an end, Emily was quickly surrounded by many well-wishers. She stayed and ate lunch in the lunchroom, which gave many additional students opportunities to chat with her. It was a great day, a new beginning. It was time for Emily to get back to school.

Emily wasn't the only person that captured my heart. My many hours in this home allowed me to get to know and develop a wonderful relationship with her entire family. It quickly became evident to me why Emily was so astounding; her entire family was. The interaction among family members touched my heart. Emily's dad was a pastor at a local church, and Emily's mom, well, to describe her accurately would require a book in and of itself. I'll just say that she is the godliest woman I have ever been privileged to call my friend. Emily's faith in God came as no surprise as I realized that this faith and belief in God had been nurtured within this family her entire life. Despite their tremendous faith, they each took the reality of Emily's blindness so hard, asking, as we all do, in tragic situations. "Why?" "Why Emily?" and "Where is God in all of this?" Each one had to find their own answers; some are still struggling with this. As for Emily, she already knows. Why? Because she invited God to use her to bring others closer to Him when she first started high school. "Where is God in all of this?" She will tell you that He has been holding her hand every step of the way.

High school proved to be a tremendous challenge not just for Emily but to all who were directly involved in her education. Many accommodations needed to be put into place to give her the assistance that she would require. Emily had two new classes added to her schedule; classes in which she would never receive credit but classes she desperately needed; braille and travel. Braille would allow her the opportunity to both read and write, a skill that is very important not just in the classroom but in many facets of living. Travel would give her a sense of independence as she learned to go from place to place. Emily was slow to embrace these two new classes. In her mind, soon she would not be in need of these skills. Growing up in a faith-filled, Spirit-filled home and church, she was confident that as everyone was praying for the restoration of her sight, she would soon be blessed with that miracle. She did work diligently, however, in all of her other classes.

When she returned to school, we quickly discovered that a student in the class could assist Emily more readily than the adult aide that was with her. The students understood the lessons being taught and could communicate that to Emily. Emily sat in the back of my room at a table and a student had already volunteered to assist Emily. It wasn't long before numerous students wanted to sit at the table, and it became evident that Emily was actually tutoring them. I recall one of the students in the front of the room asked me a question about how to decide which trigonometric formula to use to solve a certain problem. Emily, not realizing that the question was addressed to me, spoke up and said, "Wouldn't you use law of cosine because we know the length of two sides and an included angle?" Everyone, me included, looked back at the table where Emily was sitting, and we were totally blown away. I broke the silence asking jokingly if she were really blind, questioning how could she give us an answer without seeing the drawing. She stated, "You don't get it. The way you described the drawing, I really can see it." No, she couldn't see, but she was so attentive. Knowing that she had to listen for ever detail, she often saw things that others didn't.

Emily's old friends remained aloof and continued to distance themselves, and perhaps they were intimidated. On the other hand, her new friends were totally mesmerized by Emily's candor, attitude, intelligence, and amazing personality.

After being in this class for several months, I shared with Emily that I wish she could get a glimpse of students' reactions as she responded to questions, added to discussions, tutored other students, and offered her occasional snide little remarks. I explained that the personality of the entire group had changed since she entered in January. Overall grades had improved and everyone enjoyed coming to class. Her presence and her success in this class had motivated and inspired all these students to do a better job. Emily was not originally scheduled to be in this class. She was a sophomore and these students were freshman. Because I had been tutoring Emily all along, the administration honored my request to continue teaching her.

Emily also renewed an active roll in key club. She especially enjoyed going to the parties at the nursing home. She would assist in serving the party food and then go around and visit with many of the residents. Like so many others, these residents were amazed by Emily's positive attitude, willingness to be of service and her never ending smile.

Emily's birthday was in early May, and this class wanted to have a surprise birthday party for her. She missed school one day due to a doctor's appointment, which gave us the perfect opportunity to make preparations for this event. Cake, ice cream, party food was the easy part to plan; it was the gift that baffled us. What to give to a blind girl at her sweet sixteen birthday party? It had to be special; it had to be from the heart. With the money we collected, we purchased earrings that dangled the South Carolina palm tree and crescent moon that she would be able to distinguish by touch. The gift from the heart? Everyone wrote letters to Emily describing how she had inspired them and changed their lives. I encouraged many teachers and other students to add to this collection, and they were placed in a small treasure chest, symbolic of the treasure she was to us. That evening, a very emotional mother read each of the letters to her daughter. The letters were later typed and placed in a file folder, on her computer, that was capable of actually reading them to her. So on those rare occasions, when the struggle seemed too difficult and Emily would begin to wonder if she really was making a difference, those letters were a constant reminder of just a few of the many lives she was influencing.

Emily did not simply complete high school; she did it with many honors and accolades. She received the coveted Principal's Award, which is given to an outstanding senior displaying character, citizenship, scholarship, and service. She ranked tenth in her class and in addition was awarded several scholarships.

This tremendous accomplishment brought on many more questions. College? She reiterated the fact that she always wanted to be a teacher, and that desire didn't diminish with the loss of her sight. I shared with her that whether she knew it or not, that desire had already become a reality. She teaches us every day the importance of a positive attitude, to never give up, and that life's many obstacles do not keep us from our goals but make us stronger for the journey. I told her that her classroom is not going to be confined to four walls in a school building; her future, wherever it takes her, will be her classroom.

For college to be a reality, Emily and her parents decided that she needed to learn independent-living skills. So a week after graduation, Littleton, Colorado, became her new residence, and the Colorado Center for the Blind was her next challenge. Upon Emily's arrival, she was expected to cook, clean, and do her own laundry. Her first attempt at breakfast was disappointing. Due to her inability to see or smell, she poured dish soap onto her waffles rather than the maple syrup that was close by. The similarities in the shape of the bottles along with the texture of their contents were easily confused and very distasteful. Lesson learned! Mark the bottles.

This new experience was extremely difficult for Emily. The distance from home was certainly a factor, but there was so much to learn. Emily's short-term memory issues continued to impede her progress, both with travel and such things as braille. Travel techniques were very different than what she learned initially and proved to be very problematic for months. Switching techniques created confusion, which caused judgment impairments in manipulating curbs, cracks in sidewalks, driveways, and any irregularity in pavement, always with the same consequence—falling to her knees. She fell so many times that her knees were always skinned, bruised, or bleeding. She joked about needing kneepads, and for a while, she actually did wear them. However, the constant falls were far from funny; they were humiliating and painful—a constant reminder that she had so much to learn, and this journey was so demanding.

Emily never gave up. She arose from every fall a little

stronger than before. She became more determined to succeed. Braille was extremely challenging, but she knew she needed the skills that this center taught to even contemplate attending college. Graduating from the center for the blind was imperative.

Emily spent nearly a year at this center. Each month brought a new level of confidence in her ability to navigate and meet each of the demanding requirements. When Emily left home that June, she would not have ventured from her front porch alone. Now, she lived in an apartment, did all her own cooking, cleaning, laundry, grocery shopping, and travel. By travel, I mean she walked from her apartment to the bus stop, took the bus to the Denver Light Rail System, simply referred to as the rail; from there she would take the rail to school. This rail stop was several blocks from the school. Then she would navigate those final blocks to the center.

Graduation requirements seemed quite challenging even for a sighted person; hard to believe that a relatively new blind person could accomplish the demanding tasks. A three-course meal was to be prepared for seventy people. This meal was to be served at the graduation ceremony for all students, teachers, and guests who would be in attendance. Emily was to provide the menu, along with recipes, for the massive amount of food that needed to be prepared. She was to do the grocery shopping and take all items to the center where she, in a solo effort, would prepare this feast for the masses.

There were two major travel requirements for graduation.

The first was simply referred to as "The Drop." This task proved to be simple in name only. She was driven to an unknown location, dropped off, and required to find her way back to the center. The second daunting task was to complete the "Monster Route." This route consisted of traveling to four cities in the Denver area that she had never visited before. She was to travel the rail system and visit a location within each city. She had to reveal her plans of which cities and specific locations within the cities so her excursion would not simply be whatever establishment she might happen to stumble into.

Emily graduated from the center in mid-May, almost exactly eleven months after first arriving there. I was thrilled to be able to travel with Janet to attend the graduation ceremony of her daughter. The ceremony was very emotional as one after another spoke of Emily's accomplishments—her proficiency in braille, both reading and writing, and the speed in which she did so. Each teacher spoke of their pride in her dedication, drive, determination, and her amazing spirit. They spoke of Emily's incredible transformation to independence. At the completion of the ceremony, Emily was handed the Bell of Freedom, which was symbolic of her newly acquired skills, which would allow her to move forward, free to pursue any goal that she desired. As Emily jubilantly rang the bell, tears flowed from her mom, friends, peers, and teachers alike. Emily had worked so hard for this moment; she had come a long way in her quest for independence.

Emily came home for the summer but decided that she wanted to return to Denver to attend college at Metro State University. She had made numerous friends in that area, and she had become quite comfortable using the public transportation, on which she was so dependent, that this city offered.

However, familiarity with travel didn't really minimize the new difficult challenges of college. She had little trouble traveling to the college, but once there, was a different story. At first, the ability to maneuver about a college campus of this size; find classroom buildings, administrative offices, library, tutoring center, and food court as needed seemed impossible. However, Emily was never far from a stranger who was eager to assist in altering her wayward direction or even walking her to her next destination.

And then there were the classes! She took the minimal course load requirements for full-time status. It had been a year since she was in this type of classroom setting and thought best to ease back into it slowly. In two classes, she was able to do quite well; the other two required much memorization for testing, and once again her short-term memory deficiency proved to make studying tremendously difficult. Emily's teachers were extremely helpful in making much-needed accommodations to assist in Emily's success with these classes. Help from her teachers and family proved to be invaluable in that first semester.

Emily approached her second semester of school with a much different attitude, along with trying new study and note-taking techniques. This semester was to be different; she chose to take these classes without the assistance of others who proved to be an invaluable asset the first semester. This semester she was flying solo. She was determined to discover if she was capable of achieving this difficult task on her own. She literally gave this challenge all that she had, knowing if she was not successful in this endeavor that God had something else in mind for her. She once shared with me that of all the problems that the brain tumor had caused, if she could just have one thing restored, she would want it to be her memory.

Well it became apparent to Emily that God did indeed want her to stay in school. The hours and hours of revising notes, converting braille notes from class to study notes on the computer, the tremendous amount of time studying for each quiz and test all had a wonderful payload. Emily finished her first year of college with a 3.39 GPA. She is changing her major to speech with hopes of becoming a motivational speaker and perhaps even a speechwriter.

Before completing her second semester, I knew that Emily would be traveling home for her approaching spring break. I called and asked if she would be interested in talking to the senior class at the high school where I was currently teaching. She quickly and enthusiastically said yes, that she would love to tell her story to this group. I was quite astounded by the excitement in her response. My mind quickly raced back to the first time I made such a request, when a very shy, timid, doubt-filled young lady said yes. I shared with my principal my desire to have Emily speak to this group of students, and he seemed as excited as she did.

The day of the assembly arrived, and the seniors filled the gymnasium bleachers, not sure what to expect. Students, not realizing that Emily was blind, began listening intently to her story. Emily spoke so eloquently and with such confidence. Emily had spoken numerous times to large crowds but always with the assistance of her mom. Emily and Janet were a wonderful motivating team as they often shared Emily's story, but this time was different. Emily spoke alone, and Emily had a new story to tell—a story of achievement, a story of moving forward, a story of embracing the most difficult challenges and finding strength in doing so. As her story evolved and the realization of her blindness was discovered, the students were in utter amazement and disbelief. She told of her struggles, she shared the many challenges and the need to move away from home to acquire the independence that she so much needed to move forward. Every person in the gym was emotional, and tears streamed down the cheeks of many as she began her conclusion.

She proclaimed that her story was not shared for sympathy but rather for encouragement, because everyone has a story. She went on that life takes us on a journey with many obstacles and stopping at them should not be an option; working through them makes us stronger for the next. She stated that we all have choices to make; we can choose to be miserable, depressed, and simply give up, or we can choose to be happy and continue to live life to the fullest. She said either way, we are still in that circumstance, either way she is still blind. She proclaimed, "I choose to be happy and live my life to the fullest!" She said that on occasion when she might get down and life seems a bit overwhelming, she finds strength in the Scriptures, and her favorite is Philippians 4:13 (NKJV), "I can do all things through Christ who strengthens me." She concluded, "It really doesn't matter whether you believe in God or not, he still believes in you."

Emily had expressed to me months earlier that if her blindness made a difference in the life of just one person, all her struggles, all her challenges, all of her difficulties would somehow be worth it. Well, she must have felt it was worth it one hundred times over as she was flooded with the emotions of her young audience, as one after another approached her after her talk and shared how Emily inspired them to be better people; others felt like suddenly their life was worth living. Emily's talk put their challenges into a new perspective. Many lives were touched, many lives were changed; some maybe for just a few minutes, but others, I believe, for a lifetime.

I asked Emily if she still prayed for that miracle. She responded, "Yes, I do. However, I have altered it a little. I now pray that if the miracle is not mine to have, perhaps I can be that miracle for others."

Kids these days!

"I will not die; but live, and tell the works of the Lord."

(Psalm 118:17 NASB)

Perseverance

Jade was only a junior in high school when she received devastating, life-challenging news. She had been successful in many areas in her young life—honor roll, band, cheerleading, Key Club, Beta Club, National Honor Society, church. She was intelligent, dependable, athletic, involved, lived with a purpose, set high goals, always challenging herself to do her best in everything.

It was early in the school year as she was beginning her eleventh-grade year that Jade noticed a tremendous change physically. She began to tire easily, her joints began to ache often to the point she couldn't even stand, in addition to suddenly having weight-loss issues. She ignored these symptoms thinking they would simply go away as she struggled to continue with her normal activities. She ignored them until she could ignore them no longer.

Through many months and numerous trips to various doctors, Jade and her family were left with more questions than answers until through extensive and exhaustive testing it was finally discovered that Jade had lupus. At this age, a young girl's biggest concern is typically getting the perfect dress for the prom. However, for Jade, the realization of this disease quickly changed her focus to survival.

Lupus is an autoimmune disease which causes one's immune system to attack the body's otherwise-normal healthy organs and tissues. There is no cure for lupus, but it can be controlled in most people with proper medication and health care. That became the task—to find the proper medications. Jade spent much of her junior and senior years of high school in and out of the hospital, in severe pain, as this disease attacked her joints as well as continuously compromising her blood platelet levels. She discovered that low platelet levels could cause internal bleeding, severe fatigue, skin rashes, and even death.

Jade was robbed of the ability to participate in the many activities that she just a few months earlier had enjoyed and had totally taken for granted. Marching band and competitive cheerleading were out of the question. Even the routine of attending school was a challenge that was often interrupted with hospitals stays.

Keeping up with schoolwork was difficult, to say the least, but Jade never used her illness as an excuse to not perform. In fact, poor grades were not an option that Jade even entertained; she simply worked harder than ever to maintain her excellent GPA. Her education exceeded that of her peers, as she wanted to know everything possible about this new intruder that was threatening her very existence.

As Jade's senior year was winding down, she had a major flare-up and was back in the hospital. It was only a few days before the prom and her friends, realizing that

Jade would not be able to attend, made arrangements with family and nurses and surprised Jade on prom night as they brought the prom to her. Dozens of her friends showed up at the hospital in formals and festive decorations from the prom and quickly transformed the nurses' lounge for the party. Jade's mom had brought her formal to the hospital. Shocked and excited, Jade quickly changed and joined everyone for the festivities.

The severity of this flare-up caused intense pain in the joints in her legs and rendered Jade nearly immobile. This episode forced Jade to be wheelchair-bound for weeks. As graduation approached, Jade was determined to participate in the ceremony; she was going to walk across the stage unassisted to receive her diploma, as every other graduate would do. The tears flowed and applause filled the gymnasium that night as she did just that. Jade's sheer determination and courage allowed her to not only complete high school and graduate with her class; she did so with many honors and special recognitions.

The hospital stays became less frequent as physicians were finally able to stabilize Jade's condition which allowed her the opportunity to graduate college. Through much prayer, soul searching, and guidance of others, Jade has recently decided to start an organization that reaches out to victims of lupus. This is an organization to encourage, inspire, educate, and walk with those who have struggled as she had.

Jade made a conscience decision in her young adult

life that rather than allow lupus to control her, she was going to control it. She came to the realization that she had nothing in which to be ashamed. This disease would not deteriorate her character or diminish her as a person. These are the most important obstacles Jade was able to overcome; and through her newly founded organization, she is anxious to assist others in overcoming them as well.

Kids these days!

> "But those who trust in the Lord will find new strength. They will soar high on wings like eagles. They will run and not grow weary. They will walk and not faint."

> (Isaiah 40:31 NLT)

Jihad was in the tenth grade when I met him. He was in my sophomore math class. It was several days before I actually noticed that he was wearing a prosthetic arm. This was new to me. I have had numerous students with a variety of physical handicaps; but in my nearly four decades of teaching, this was the first time I had an amputee. Jihad, who prefers being called Jay, was a first.

After several weeks, and the newness of the beginning of another school year was diminishing, the students became more comfortable with their new classmates. I overheard several times students inquiring about Jay's arm and asked him how it worked. One day, as the class period was coming to an end and the students were packing up their belongings getting ready to go to their next class, one of the students felt more comfortable asking Jay that same question that many of us had: "What happened to your arm?" I listened inquisitively as he said, "A shark bit it off!" The bell rang and the class was dismissed. Everyone exited in utter amazement. Jay must have seen the astonished look on my face as he delayed leaving so he could explain. "The shark story just sounds so much better than what really happened," he declared as he smiled. He went on to share the real story.

Jay was an infant when he lost his arm. He suffered from chicken pox and strep throat simultaneously when he was one year old. Apparently the combination of the two problems created a flesh-eating bacterium. This bacterium attacked Jay's entire left side. Jay has extensive scars on his leg, side, and arm, which are constant reminders of this devastating ordeal that he really has no memory. Surgery was performed to remove the dead scar tissue, but his arm could not be saved. It was amputated just above his elbow.

Jay later shared with me that his arm was not the only thing he lost at that young age. His mother, unable to cope with the maiming of her son, abandoned her firstborn child and his father.

I was inquisitive about the meaning of the name "Jihad" because of all the negative implications that it has in today's world. Looking it up, I discovered, simply put, jihad means "struggle." Now that seems rather prophetic.

Throughout the school year, Jay has been very patient with my numerous questions as to how he performs day-to-day tasks that we all give very little thought—tasks such as trimming his fingernails, washing his hand, tying his shoes, wondering if he can swim...

At times some of the students in this class would challenge me about my inquisitive questioning of Jay; they feared that I was embarrassing him. Jay overheard the comments and quickly came to my defense. He shared that he much preferred and even appreciated the fact that I wondered about and questioned his many challenges. He said that was far better than those people who would simply stare at him as though he was not human.

I was comfortable with my relationship with Jay and I knew he was comfortable with his handicap. His own attitude about his handicap made it very easy to ask him numerous questions, and I wanted this class to witness the exchange. On this day, however, Jay was the teacher and his lesson to us all was invaluable. I began wondering how many times I had caught the eye of someone who was handicapped and found it easier to turn my head rather than engage in conversation because it might be a little awkward or uncomfortable for me. My prayer was that each one of us would have a renewed vision—eyes that see the person rather than the handicap—whenever we encounter someone who is challenged with physical or mental abnormalities.

Jay, like most young men his age, loves sports. However, he is not content with just being a spectator. Jay wants to play! Jay finds a way to play!

Jay tried out for the high school JV basketball team and actually made the cut. He was thrilled that he made the team. However, he was unable to play because of transportation issues for practices. The sport he enjoys the most is baseball. In the spring, he competed for a spot on the JV team but this time came up short. Coach told him he had a lot of talent and that it came down between him and another guy, "But don't give up," the coach encouraged. Jay is determined to eventually be on the team, and he dedicates long hours in batting cages to continue to improve his batting skills.

One Monday morning, before school, I saw Jay in the commons area as he approached me with a grin that you could see in his eyes. He exclaimed, "You'll never guess what I did this weekend!" Then I suggested that perhaps he share it with me. As he was speaking, his best friend, Justin, approached us and joins in the conversation. Jay was thrilled that Justin took him to play golf. It was his very first attempt at this sport, and he relinquished that he was not very good. Justin quickly spoke up sharing that Jay actually hit the pin on one of his drives, and Jay just smiled. They both laughed as they relived their adventure on the golf course.

Justin is arguably Jay's best friend. You don't see one without the other close by. Justin and Jay are in my same math class. They sit one in front of the other, directly in front of my desk. On those rare occasions, when I can actually sit at my desk during class, we often engage in conversation. As the year evolved, so had my knowledge of these young men's stories. I began to understand why there was such a bond between the two. Justin, too, had suffered a devastating loss.

Unlike Jay's, Justin's loss was not so visibly evident. Justin shared with me that one year before entering high school, he lost his mom. His parents were divorced, and with joint custody, Justin spent much time in both homes. He and his mom were extremely close. Like Jay, Justin loved sports. He ran track and played baseball but never without his mom in the stands cheering him on.

One evening, when Justin was staying with his dad, the man that his mom was contemplating marrying murdered her. Justin shared that this man had a drinking problem, and when he drank he often became abusive. On this particular evening, apparently an argument ensued and so did his violent temper. This man, whom she loved and trusted, got a knife from the kitchen and brutally stabbed her to death. Justin awoke the next morning to the horrible news as his dad and other family members gathered to comfort one another.

Justin's mom's voice was silenced on that dreadful evening due to senseless domestic violence; it was silenced to everyone except Justin. He articulated that he deals with his loss through his participation in sports, specifically cross country and baseball. He went on to say that he can actually feel her presence and sometimes hear her voice of encouragement as he competes. He stated that it is hard to explain, but her presence is very real to him. Justin is very competitive and as a freshman broke school records in cross-country as well as track-and-field. He was region champ in his sophomore year and finished fifth in the state championship meet. Justin went on to be named cross-country runner of the year for our area.

In Justin's own words from his post on Facebook:
"Two years ago today my mom's beautiful life was taken from me and many others. A few days before her death, I overheard her say that she thinks I'll be a runner when I'm older. To this day, I am always motivated to make that happen and make her proud of me. That's why I push myself everyday I'm out there on the trail, course, or track. A lot of people ask me how I'm so fast and how can I run so well and not stop when I get tired. In response, I usually say, "I don't know," but on the inside, I really know it's because I really want her dream to come true and for me, it's my way of showing her how much I love her. And to answer how I keep going when I'm tired...I always keep her with me and I'm always wearing her angel wings. When I get tired in the middle of a race, I start praying and praying over and

over, knowing my mom is there with me and guiding me through the race. She is the reason why I don't stop. One day, I hope to make it to the Olympics, for my mom, which is my ultimate goal in life. Winning a medal is not my goal, making it there is all I want, even though a medal would be pretty nice. My second life goal for you, Mom, is to earn first place in a 26.2. And throughout my life, I'm dedicating my entire running career to you, Mom. RIP MGW"

The summer prior to Justin's sophomore year, there was a 5K run held as a fundraising event for a local girl who lost multiple limbs due to a flesh-eating bacteria she contracted during a zip-line accident. Justin won that race along with the prize money in which he immediately returned to the girl's father to assist with the expenses she continues to accrue in her recovery efforts. The father tearfully embraced Justin as he accepted Justin's generous gift.

Justin and Jay were friends in grade school, and they renewed their friendship when they entered high school. Perhaps unknowingly drawn together, they were different when they entered high school; they had so much more in common than ever before. These two young men have a much different perspective of life than that of their peers. They have seen and experienced far more tragedy than most ever will. They don't take life for granted. "Can't" and "quit" are words that do not exist in their vocabulary. Together they move forward, encouraging one another, challenging one another, dreaming of future goals with a bond stronger than that of blood—it is a bond of genuine brotherhood.

Kids these days!

> "We are afflicted in every way, but not crushed; perplexed, but not despairing; persecuted, but not forsaken; struck down, but not destroyed;"
> (2 Corinthians 4: 8–9 NASB)

Melissa was excited about life. She had just celebrated her seventeenth birthday ten days prior; Thanksgiving was a wonderful recent memory as thoughts moved forward toward the anticipation of the Christmas holidays. *Life is good,* she thought as she crawled into bed that evening.

As a new day dawned, Melissa was awakened to devastating news. Life as Melissa had once known it would never be the same. Melissa's dad revealed to her that her mother had passed away. He had awakened in the early hours of the morning and noticed his wife was not in bed. When he arose to check about her, he quickly discovered her lifeless body. Nothing about her death made sense until an autopsy revealed that Melissa's mom had coronary artery disease in which no one was aware.

Overnight, Melissa's role at home transformed from "princess" to caregiver. Melissa had two brothers—one five years older and the second ten years younger. As the family attempted to move forward, it just seemed natural that Melissa, being the only female in the house, would take on all the duties of "Mom." Melissa was quickly forced into an unfamiliar role with tremendous challenges.

At the funeral, her younger brother, still quite confused about all that had happened, looks to Melissa tearfully and asks if she would be his new mom. Melissa promised him at that moment that she would indeed be his new mom. These words were not spoken to appease that young child for the moment, not simply an empty promise. This was a commitment from her heart. From that point on, everything and everybody would take a backseat to her little brother. Even Melissa's boyfriend understands this special relationship, this amazing bond.

I didn't know Melissa until I had her in my senior math class. What I saw was a beautiful young lady, always smiling, great attitude, quiet demeanor, quick to tutor others when they needed assistance with newly learned material. I only learned of Melissa's story in the spring of that school year. She kind of reminds me of a duck sitting on the water; on the surface you see a calm, beautiful, quiet creature, gliding across the water. However, if you take a peek beneath the surface, you'll see a different picture—that duck is paddling like mad to get to the other side.

Melissa's life has to be demanding with responsibilities both at school and at home, but I have never heard her complain, never heard her make excuses about not performing, never contemplating giving up. Melissa is a wonderful student with a great GPA and plans on attending college with aspirations of being a nurse.

In the spring of her senior year, with the help of her dad, Melissa held a very successful car show in memory of her mom with proceeds going to the American Heart Association. She raised over $600 with this fundraiser and plans to make it an annual event in hopes of next year being bigger and better than the last.

Melissa tearfully shared that on Mother's Day her little brother insisted that their dad buy flowers for her because, "She is my mom!" A very emotional Melissa was extremely grateful for the thoughtful gift.

As the school year was winding down and everyone was preparing for final exams, Melissa was absent from my class. Concerned, I inquired about her absence with her friend. She shared that Melissa's little brother had a bad asthma attack and had to be hospitalized. Melissa spent the night with him and the next morning left the hospital only to come to school and begin taking exams.

The seniors were anxiously sharing their college plans, with many leaving home to continue their education. I knew Melissa wanted to be a nurse as I inquired as to the college she would be attending. She quickly responded, "Oh, I'm staying home to attend college." She smiled confidently. She was comfortable with her decision because nearly a year and a half ago she made a promise to a young man that she would be his mom. She learned so young in life that life is not about us, rather how we can be of service to others. She is a strong Christian woman who is an amazing role model to many.

Kids these days!

"Blessed is the man who perseveres under trial, because when he has stood the test, he will receive the crown of life that God has promised to those who love him."

(James 1:12 NIV)

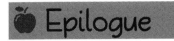 **Epilogue**

In Their
Own Words

Shortly after completing the final chapter of this book, the school year was rapidly coming to a close. It was exam week and on this particular morning I had no students scheduled for the testing sessions. Quite *coincidentally* and for various reasons, Troy (chapter 10), Emily (chapter 11), Justin, Jay and Melissa (chapter 12) were all in my classroom together.

At first it was just Jay and Emily. I brought Emily to school with me, she was home from college and was in hopes of "seeing" some of the seniors whom she had met when she gave her talk a couple of months prior. Jay came into my room to show off his prosthetic arm, which had just been repaired. Jay immediately recognized Emily and began explaining to her the mechanics of his artificial limb. She felt his hand with hers as he manipulated the fingers and began spinning his hand 360 degrees.

Troy showed up shortly after that to discuss an event he was planning and quickly settled in and made himself at home. After introductions and much small talk, Troy questioned Jay, "So what is your story?" As Jay was relating some intimate details, Troy asked if he had ever been bullied. With Jay's affirmation to the question, they each shared how they dealt with similar problems. Moments later, Jay talked about playing golf. Once again Troy interjects a simple question, "How?" Jay quickly responds so matter of factly, "With one arm!" Troy laughed and said maybe he should try that approach perhaps that could help his golf game. Emily chimed in from several seats away saying, "Go ahead and close your eyes while you're at it; that's the way I play!" Everyone enjoyed the candidness of the responses.

After morning test, Justin and Melissa came in to look over final editing of their sections in my book. Melissa, recognizing Emily went directly to her and they chatted as though they were long time friends. Justin sat with the guys as they spoke one common language, sports. Justin and Troy had much in common, both being very successful in track.

I leaned back in my chair with tears in my eyes relishing what was happening. Never in my wildest dreams did I ever contemplate that these young people would even meet, not to mention that they would actually have an opportunity to share their stories, their trials and their successes with one another.

It was then that I realized that the chapters could continue to be written...every year...every class. I continue to discover kids facing overwhelming challenges, looking beyond themselves, drawing strength from God, family and friends, not giving up, not making excuses. They ultimately become stronger as they embrace their challenge and continue in their quest to achieve their goals. These students, and so many more, have been a tremendous influence on me. I am inspired by their courage and conviction. I am motivated by their strength and fortitude. Most importantly, I am proud and feel extremely privileged that I have had the opportunity to have a front row seat as I witnessed the transformation of tragedy to triumph as these young people refuse to be defeated. I can boastfully exclaim that I am a better person for having had the pleasure of teaching *Kids These Days* for the past forty years.

> "Consider it pure joy, my brothers and sisters, whenever you face trials of many kinds because you know that the testing of your faith produces perseverance. Let perseverance finish its work so that you may be mature and complete, not lacking anything."
>
> (James 1: 2-4 NIV)

I have told these kids' stories and how it has impacted my life. Now I want to give you the opportunity to hear from them.

In Their Own Words...

It is amazing to be able to look back at past events, like that Christmas assembly and then the motivational talk to the seniors at Mary Thomas' high school, and to be able to see how far God has brought me. One thing I have learned is that God is always near to us, even when He feels distant. The Bible says that, "He will never leave us or forsake us, even if we walk through the valley of the shadow of death". This has been proven true to me in so many different ways.

When life seems impossible and you see no way out of the most difficult circumstances, I challenge you to walk by faith, for then you will not be walking alone. Besides, walking by sight can be deceptive, and so overrated. ☺

Emily Zimmermann (Chapter 11)

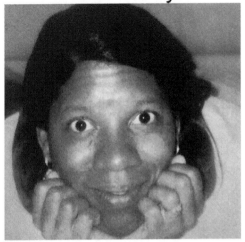

Life for me was full of many trials that made me feel like I had no voice. I used the game of basketball to help me express my emotions and passion. As I matured I learned that basketball was a game that should not be used in place of relationships and self-expression. Once I was able to speak about my fears and anger the game of basketball became secondary in my life. I had to learn that my past was my past but I had a purpose and a presence.

I could have just given up when people made fun of me because of where I lived. I could have given up when people teased me about my short stature. Giving up would have been too easy, expected, typical and total failure. I wanted to do more, see more and go further than expected. I prayed to God to help me and He did. My transformation started internally but its rewards could be seen externally. DON'T QUIT!

"Love is patient, love is kind. It does not envy, it does not boast, it is not proud.

It does not dishonor others, it is not self-seeking, it is not easily angered, it keeps no record of wrongs."

(1Corinthians 13:4-5 NIV)

Tina Desper Law (Chapter 3)

Growing up the way I did made me the man that I am today. All the struggles made me work harder for what I wanted. I learned that struggles are a blessing in disguise; it just depends on how you choose to handle it. You can run from it or run through it. I chose to run through it. Here I am today a blessed man of God, husband, father, mentor, business owner, and so much more to come. Run through your struggle.

Troy Williamson (Chapter 10)

When I was younger I remember being angry and embarrassed about missing an arm. I was often bullied and made fun of in middle school. However, over time I have come to realize that I have no control of the thoughts of others, but I can control mine. As I began to accept my handicap for what it was, I realized that I am no different than others. What I once perceived to be a handicap was in reality, my strength.

Yes, I may have some limitations, but those limitations inspire me to strive harder in life to accomplish those things that most people would think impossible with just one arm. I had to work much harder than others to make the cut on the JV basketball team and my goal now is to be on my school's baseball team. I know in my heart that I can do and be anything I want if I'm willing to work for it.

I know that there will always be those who stare and only see what's missing in my life; I prefer to focus on those, like a young boy at baseball camp this summer, who did not have a hand. When he watched me play, what he saw was hope and inspiration.

One of my favorite quotes is from Friedrich Nietzsche, "What doesn't kill us makes us stronger."

Jihad Shakur (Chapter 12)

There were times when I knew my life was spiraling out of control and I felt so helpless. But, every single time, God brought someone special into my life to help me get through the tough times. He constantly reminds me that I am never alone, that He, sometimes through other people, always walks beside me.

This is what encourages me to reach out to others in need. When someone feels that their burden is too heavy to carry, and God seems so far away, I pray that I can be His physical presence to them and help lighten their load. Through my many challenges God has gifted me with a giving and serving heart. Life is a gift and we need to be that gift to others.

Benita Bandy (Chapter 2)

When my wonderful mother's life was taken, I was extremely devastated and for awhile I was lost, feeling alone in this world. Finding myself again took some time because I repeatedly asked, "Why me?" God finally answered one day. He reminded me that everything happens for a reason and that is when I realized that He chose me because I have the strength and perseverance to get through it. I was then sure of what I needed to do, which is to be successful in life and to pursue my dreams while honoring my mother in the process. Romans 5:3-4 says, "We rejoice in our sufferings because we know that suffering produces perseverance; perseverance, character, and character, hope." This one verse says so much, and it is what I will always live by for eternity. Running is the one thing that helps me overcome my sufferings and it also is what my mother wanted me to do with my life. The following is a poem that I wrote that keeps me focused in life and I hope and pray it helps to inspire others dealing with adversity to also stay focused and have hope.

As God says, Hope never fails,
For in my life I will prevail;
And as God's hand controls my fate,
In heaven does my treasure await.

Justin Weegar (Chapter 12)

The events of 9/11 have changed my life forever. As a senior in high school, I knew, without a doubt, that life was all about ME. However, I never felt so helpless as I did on that Tuesday morning as I watched with other classmates the devastation of that terrorist attack. As a volunteer fireman, I kept feeling like I need to do something. Reaching out to the York family was the beginning of a changing heart within me. I don't believe that I ever felt so proud about doing something for someone else.

I would like to take this opportunity to thank all firefighters and those serving in our military. I have tremendous respect for these people who willingly put their lives on the line for others; who willingly go into harms way to serve and protect. I think of their sacrifice often, as I am able to be with my young children after a hard day's work and our deployed military is half a world away from their loved ones.
Thank you for your service!

Bradley Crawford (Chapter 9)

Life is about choices. To understand yourself, you must recognize that life is about the choices you make mentally, physically, spiritually, emotionally, and socially. Before my diagnosis, I did not appreciate many of the simple things that God had blessed me with. However, when your life is constantly being tested, you begin to look at the world differently. The smallest things become the most important. For example, shopping and cheerleading were priorities on my list, but after experiencing so much with my health, me being able to walk became extremely important to me. You may wonder why walking? But until the ability is taken from you, you will never begin to appreciate how major being able to walk is.

I started embracing every aspect of my life. Most importantly, I started embracing the person God meant for me to become. I made the choice to be a fighter! I had Lupus, but I had to make sure not only had I known that, but those who encountered me. I could have fallen into depression or pitied myself, but I chose not to. The key to becoming a fighter is willingly making the decision that obstacles do not characterize the individual.... The actions made by the individual after the obstacle is encountered are what create his/her character.

You must challenge yourself to continuously embrace the choice to maintain and possess joy and happiness. Life will happen, but it takes a fighter to choose to overcome adversity and the challenges that will be met along the journey. Never allow your obstacles to define who you are! For me, I realized at a younger age that God has blessed me too much for me to allow life to defeat me.

Am I saying the ability to make that choice comes easy? No, by no means am I! But I am saying that you have to pray for the courage to make the choice to choose positivity in your life no matter the given circumstances. Lupus may hinder me at some points, but it does not control me. The only thing I allowed Lupus to do was to make me stronger so that I could continue encouraging and building others.

My favorite personal quote is: "Be the change you want to see." I made up in my mind that in order to seek a positive change in your life, you must "be that change." Once you start becoming that change, you have already made the choice to lead your life under God's purpose and promise for you.

Through my drive to continuously encourage other

people, I have accomplished more than what many expected from me. I graduated from one of the most prestigious Mass Communications programs in the nation! I recently embarked on the journey of pursuing my doctoral degree in physical therapy while working a full time job. Furthermore, I started my own campaign called ROYAL. Under my campaign, we embrace the theme to "Give Lupus Royal Treatment." I travel across South Carolina educating teenagers and adults on Lupus Awareness, while hosting fundraisers for Lupus research. I raised over $3,000 in four weeks! But my journey doesn't stop there! I have been fortunate enough to travel and meet other Lupus advocates. And last but not least, I am now on the board of directors for a nonprofit group in South Carolina geared to helping the lives of Lupus survivors run smoothly financially and physically.

I leave you with this: Be the change you want to see. Make the choice to not allow adversity or obstacles to defeat you in your journey to unveiling your purpose. Allow God to lead you in the path he sees fit for you.

Jade Nealious (Chapter 12)

The person I am today and who I was as a high school student is a direct reflection of the people who influenced me the most in my life. I have been truly blessed with parents who taught me respect, responsibility and a strong work ethic; my close friends assisted in developing in me a positive, caring, giving, good-natured attitude; the teacher who taught beyond the textbook and challenged me to be a person of character, and offered me many opportunities through key club to discover the joy of reaching out and being of service to others; coaches taught me the path to success was facing and then conquering adversity. There were no short cuts; there was no victory in running away, ignoring or running around difficult situations.

Yes, I was blessed throughout my life with amazing role models; however, I believe that everyone has these positive role models as well as the negative ones within their reach. I challenge you to take a close look at those around you; do they build you up? Are you a better person because of your association with them? Is your life going in a positive direction or are your role models leading you down a path of despair?

In every circumstance in my life I still have to be the one to make the choice. The choices are not always easy, and no one makes the best choice all the time. However, making good decisions on a daily basis builds character and that strong character will aid you in making the correct decision when you are faced with life's most difficult circumstances.

The impact of the people I chose to be role models in my life, stretch beyond my chosen profession; those characteristics that they shared with me have become intertwined into the very fabric of my day to day life. It is my goal to pass on these characteristics by being a positive role model to the students and athletes that I work with today.

Matt Hayes (Chapter 8)

My days as one of Mary Thomas students' were very enlightening to say the least. I was never a trouble maker just a student trying to do the bare minimum it required to pass a class. My favorite spot in class was to sit in the back as the military saying goes "out of sight, out of mind". This saying did not work with Mrs. Thomas, it seems as if I was like a magnet that always seemed to get her attention. I was that low-key student sitting in the back of the classroom doing only what I needed to pass a class. Another reason why I was reserved in her class was my belief of how I thought others viewed me. Instead of my reservations keeping them at a distance it ended up wanting Ms. Thomas and others in the class to know more about me.

By their acceptance and not judging me based on outside appearances, in the end I figured I am a part of a team and I needed to play my part and that's just what I did. Instead of feeling helpless I became a helper. They challenged how I believed they viewed me. Even though before Ms. Thomas' class I always had the need

152

to give back to others because of my mother instilling in me that life wasn't always about me, Ms. Thomas' service learning class allowed me to see that I could really make a difference in the lives of others.

After high school I joined the US Marine Corps and traveled the world and took part in fighting for the freedom of others both here in the US and other countries. When it comes to people's perceptions of me I still tend to prove people wrong when they try to judge a book by its cover.

I learned that you should not allow your difference in background and upbringing to interfere with you attaining the same knowledge as your peers. As long as you believe in yourself, set aside your fears, and believe that you can achieve and believe you will be able to do anything you put your mind to in life. I am grateful for my experience in Ms. Thomas class as well as military service because it showed me that when I walk in a room filled with people of all backgrounds and ethnicities, I am just as worthy as they are. I no longer have pre-conceived beliefs of how someone views me I judge a man now on his actions towards me.

Twon Hickson (Chapter 7)

Losing my mom was the most difficult and unexpected tragedy I could have ever imagined happening. From that moment on, my life would forever be changed. No longer am I just a teenage girl; I've inherited the responsibilities of an adult. I had to grow up a lot faster than other girls my age. However, I've realized so much since that day, and with the comfort of God's unfailing love, I've found happiness in my circumstances. My dad and I are closer than ever and my little brother has become the center of my world. I have matured and grown in my spiritual walk. My faith in God is unshakable. Even in my weakest moment He never left my side. Isaiah 41:10 (NKJ) says, "So do not fear, for I am with you; do not be dismayed, for I am your God. I will strengthen you and help you; I will uphold you with my righteous right hand." This verse has given me comfort in the most difficult times, and I know that my mom is proud of the woman I have become.

Melissa Steves (Chapter 12)

Share Your Story...

I hope that you enjoyed reading this book as much as I did writing it. This was an incredible opportunity to reconnect with all those written about in the preceding pages. It gave me tremendous pleasure discovering that each one is doing very well all these years later.

I know that I am not the only one who has been so privileged to work with such amazing young people. We all know that those positive, "feel good" stories about kids these days do not get the recognition that they need. Here is your opportunity to change that. I would like to invite you to share your "kids these day" story with me for future editions.

Find out more on my website at
www.kidsthesedaysmct.com

I would love to hear from you.

Endorsements

It's rare that a book is written that can be so inspirational and so compelling to such a large audience. This book has an extremely important message for parents, teachers and students alike. Actually I can't think of any person who would not benefit from reading this amazing book.

In our current culture of instant gratification and the attitude of I deserve what everyone else has; it's good to read about kids who have persevered through some of life's most difficult challenges armed with nothing more than their own inner strength and convictions. I applaud them and I thank Mary Thomas for sharing them with us. It's a welcome change to read something both positive and inspirational about, "Kids these days".

— Frank Endres,
Business Owner – brother of the author

The real deal...everything you read between these covers is truly "the real deal." I began my career under the tutelage of Mary Thomas. She wasted no time enlisting me in her army to fight poor home life, as she did many other fledgling educators. She refuses to see the quit in children. She refuses to see the bad in society. Those are challenges to overcome with love. The stories in this book made me laugh. They also made me cry. Not a partial tear forming in the corner of my eye, but the kind of heaving that brings your spouse from the other room to check on you. Every story is true. Every story is accurate. Every story is its own small miracle that inspires us to give back and step up. Mary sets the bar high for her friends. She is God's tool on earth that makes us all realize we can truly make a difference. Each life changed gives back ten fold. When you read this book, you too will give back. You have no choice according to Mary J. Enjoy!

— Todd Bornscheuer, M. Ed.
Principal, H.E. McCracken Middle School

This incredible book is a must read for anyone working with kids these days. In each and every chapter is an emotion filled journey that serves as a profound reminder of the life changing power that teachers posses when working with teenagers today. Seasoned veteran Mary Thomas uses her 40 years of teaching experience to ignite a spark of motivation and determination that every single reader will feel before putting this book down. She shows us that with a tremendous passion for students' success, no matter what the circumstance, you will not fail them.

— Della Hughes, Ed.S.
Mathematics Teacher, Evans HS

What a great book for anybody who might be feeling like they are "alone" in the world. It is an inspirational delivery of stories of encouragement laced with humor, reality, and compassion. For those of us who deal with children every day, you'll recognize a set of familiar journeys that you've likely observed in your students. I found it to be a helpful reminder of the "little light that shines" in even the most trying of circumstances.

Teachers, parents and students should enjoy either a cover-to-cover reading or just picking through the chapters.

— Donald B. Brigdon, Ed.S.
Principal Evans HS

While each of the kids whose story is told in this book are truly amazing, it also has much to do with the teacher who taught them. I believe that there still may have been a story to tell, but because of Mary Thomas' support and encouragement, these kids made the choice to be above the circumstances that were present in their lives.

— Janet Zimmermann
Colorado Dept of Education

"Rarely do you meet a professional who encompasses all the traits and characteristics needed to reach the youth of today. Mary Thomas is a woman, wife, mother, daughter, sister and, without a doubt, a world-class educator with the personality and tools needed to engage young minds, the willing and sometimes unwilling. **<u>Kids These Days</u>** is a unique, yet frank testament to who sits in classrooms across the nation, and who stands before those seated everyday. The myths surrounding educators is dissolved once you finish the very first chapter of **Kids These Days**! This book not only shares true stories of remarkable kids but showcases the keen eye in which teachers view not only subject matter, but the well being of their students. This is an uplifting, powerful feel-good collection of Thomas's truths, her heroes and her view of kids these days."

— Tammie Newman
Public Information Officer
Aiken County Public Schools
former student and biggest fan of Mary Thomas ;-)

"Kids These Days" is a book written in a warm, oft times humorous, conversational style as Mary Thomas conveys to us enjoyable stories of a number of different teenagers who, under her tutelage, have grown to learn and experience the joy of looking beyond themselves and strive to become a blessing to others. This is quite an accomplishment when dealing with teenagers who have the stereotypical reputation for being, self-indulgent, self-obsessed and having a "what's in it for ME!" attitude.

Mary Thomas does a masterful job of creating for us a sampler patchwork quilt comprised of the lives of representative students covering four decades in time, male and female, of various racial backgrounds, the "haves" and "have-nots", the athletic and the disabled, the healthy and the terminally ill, from loving intact families and from severely dysfunctional families – demonstrating that these most admirable quality traits can be found living within us all waiting to be released if we but assume the right attitudes, pick the right role models and make the right choices in our lives.

I highly recommend this book not only for educators and students but also for the general public. There are lessons to be learned from this book for all readers young and old.

— Gerard G. Endres
Professional Engineer, brother of author

Mary Thomas is one of the most gifted teachers I have met in my career in education. She has the ability to truly connect with students in a way that is genuinely caring while also encouraging them to always give their very best. With this book, she weaves a fascinating story of young people who were not defined by their circumstances or the challenges they faced. It's the

161

story of the difference an individual can make in the world and a story of the power of faith in our lives. As she shares about the students who have touched her life, she is sharing a story of great hope for our future.

— Dr. Deidre M. Martin
Vice Chancellor for University Advancement
University of South Carolina Aiken
Past President of Aiken Kiwanis

Manufactured by Amazon.ca
Bolton, ON

31883717R00098